Crimson Glory

Alabama Rolls to the National Championship

Creg Stephenson

This book is available in quantity at special discounts for your group or organization.
For further information contact:

Triumph Books
542 South Dearborn Street
Suite 750
Chicago, IL 60605
Phone: (312) 939-3330
Fax: (312) 663-3557
www.triumphbooks.com

Printed in the United States of America
ISBN: 978-1-60078-425-5

All photographs courtesy of Stuart McNair unless otherwise indicated

Content packaged by Mojo Media, Inc.
Joe Funk: Editor
Jason Hinman: Creative Director

contents

Alabama Wins National Title No. 13

Alabama 37, Texas 21 • January 7, 2010 • Pasadena, California

As confetti fell all around him and chants of "Roll Tide!" echoed throughout Pasadena's Arroyo Seco, Alabama defensive end Brandon Deaderick could only shake his head in wonder at what his team had accomplished on this brisk January evening in Southern California. "To be a part of this tradition, it's amazing," Deaderick said. "We're in the history books. We're actually part of those lists of great teams at the University of Alabama. I'm so excited."

On the strength of a 37–21 victory over Texas at the Rose Bowl, Deaderick and his teammates hoisted the Coaches Trophy crystal football as college football's national champions for 2009. It was Alabama's 13th title overall, but first in 17 years.

Deaderick had not even entered elementary school when Alabama won its last championship and was more than a decade away from signing with the Crimson Tide as a member of the 2005 recruiting class. The Kentucky native has seen plenty of down times in his Alabama career, but January 7, 2010, will officially go down as the night the Crimson Tide unquestionably marked its return to the top of the college football landscape.

"It's amazing," Deaderick said. "To be at the bottom of the totem pole in the SEC (in 2006), and to make the move up and have this chance, it's just great. I can't really put it into words."

Deaderick and his teammates would let their action speak plenty loud in the BCS National Championship Game, building a 24–6 halftime lead on the strength of several big plays by the defense. They knocked Texas quarterback—and two-time Heisman Trophy finalist—Colt McCoy out of the game early on, then withstood a furious comeback by the Longhorns before putting the game away with two late touchdowns.

It was Alabama's first-ever win over Texas in 10 tries, with many of those previous losses coming in gut-wrenching fashion in bowl games. The victory also came at the site where Alabama first forged its national football reputation, having won the Rose Bowl in the championship seasons of 1925, 1930, and 1934.

"I'm happy for our fans, I'm happy for our players, I'm happy for all the people who work so hard to try to restore this," Alabama coach Nick Saban said. "And I'm very happy myself that we were able to make such a sig-

nificant contribution to something that's a pretty significant accomplishment for our organization. But I'm really happiest for all the other people, to see them so happy about what was accomplished."

Among those celebrating on the field were running backs Mark Ingram and Trent Richardson, who carried an Alabama offense that had its troubles getting a consistent passing game going. Ingram—the Heisman Trophy winner and the BCS title game Offensive Most Valuable Player—and Richardson combined for 205 yards and four touchdowns on 41 carries, as the Crimson Tide ran the ball on 51 of 63 offensive snaps.

The Crimson Tide's other touchdown came on an interception return by Alabama defensive end Marcell Dareus, who might have contributed the night's biggest play on Texas' first offensive possession. The 6-foot-4, 296-pound sophomore slammed into McCoy's right shoulder on an option run, knocking the fifth-year senior from the game and killing an early opportunity for a Longhorns touchdown.

"I wasn't even thinking about it," Dareus said of McCoy's injury. "I was just like 'I'm not going to let him get in this end zone.' Coaches always say 'don't even think, just play the game.' I didn't think, I just laid it down. I just heard a thump—my neck snapped back. I did lay it down pretty hard, though. That's just how the game goes."

Following a botched fake punt on Alabama's game-opening possession, Texas took over at the Crimson 37, but couldn't get into the end zone despite two quick first downs that moved the ball to the 11. McCoy was injured on first down and in came Garrett Gilbert, a true freshman whose only previous game experience had been in mop-up duty during the regular season.

The Longhorns kept the ball on the ground to begin with, getting another first down and scoring an apparent touchdown that was nullified because of an illegal

Trent Richardson explodes for a 49-yard touchdown against the Longhorns in the second quarter. He rushed 19 times for 109 yards.

formation. Three more Texas plays failed to score a touchdown, and Lawrence Hunter drilled an 18-yard field goal for a 3–0 Longhorns lead.

Texas used a sky kickoff—which Alabama inexplicably let hit the ground—to get the ball right back, but again could not get into the end zone. Hunter hit a 42-yarder and the Longhorns led 6–0 with 8:04 left in the opening quarter.

The two teams traded punts before the Crimson Tide finally put together a touchdown march early in the second quarter. Ingram ran three times for 26 yards to loosen up the Texas defense, and then quarterback Greg McElroy hit Julio Jones for a 23-yard gain to move the ball deep into Longhorns territory. Ingram carried the ball three straight times from there, including a 1-yard run to tie the game with 14:18 left in the second quarter. Leigh Tiffin's extra point gave Alabama 7–6 advantage, and the Crimson Tide never trailed again.

It was the run game that got Alabama back on the

(opposite) Heisman hero Mark Ingram delivered on the big stage, carrying 22 times for 116 yards and two touchdowns. (above) Meanwhile, all an injured and frustrated Colt McCoy could do was watch his team from the sideline.

Getty Images

board midway through the second quarter. This time it was Richardson who found the goal line, bursting through a gaping hole for a 49-yard touchdown and a 14–6 Alabama lead with 7:59 left before halftime.

"We only passed the ball for (58) yards," Alabama center William Vlachos said. "In a game like that, the offensive line has got to step up; the running backs have got to make plays. That's how you've got to win games like this—(against) a very physical defense, a lot of team speed. I can't say enough about the way Trent and Mark ran the ball tonight."

Alabama added Tiffin's 26-yard field goal with 29 seconds left in the half, leaving just enough time for Dareus' second—and most memorable—big play. On

second-and-1 at the Texas 37, Gilbert attempted a shovel pass to running back D.J. Monroe, but Deaderick jarred the ball loose and into the arms of Dareus, who suddenly displayed running skills that would make Ingram and Richardson jealous.

The big man first stiff-armed Gilbert to the ground and then avoided Texas tackle Kyle Hix with a spin move back inside to cap off a 28-yard touchdown that gave Alabama a 24–6 halftime lead. The tackle of McCoy and the interception were the only times Dareus showed up in the stat sheet, but they might have been the two biggest plays of the game.

"My first reaction was grab the ball, and then after that I blanked out, and all I was thinking about is Mark

(above) Richardson proved the 'Bama backfield will be a crushing and combustible force next year. (opposite) Texas backup quarterback Garrett Gilbert fumbles as he is hit by linebacker Eryk Anders. Gilbert struggled early but settled down and played a decent game against a relentless 'Bama defense.

Mark Ingram's gutty running in the fourth quarter, including this carry for a touchdown, secured the championship for the Crimson Tide.

Ingram and Javier (Arenas) and just doing moves I didn't think I could do," said Dareus, named the game's Defensive MVP. "I was like, 'I can't believe I pulled off that (spin).' I saw that lineman coming for my legs, and my first reaction was to spin. I looked to my left and I saw Eryk Anders, I knew it was a touchdown. I could not wait to get to the end zone."

Despite Alabama's commanding halftime lead, Texas was far from finished, as Gilbert finally found his passing rhythm. He connected with senior Jordan Shipley on a pair of second-half touchdowns, the second a 44-yarder that pulled Texas within three at 24–21 with 6:15 left in the game.

Alabama's offense managed only one first down on its next possession and Texas amazingly had the ball and a chance to win the game and the national championship with 3:14 to play. After the Longhorns got a quick first down on a defensive holding penalty to put the ball on their own 17, Alabama's big-play defense once again stood tall.

Senior linebacker Eryk Anders got around the corner and got to Gilbert for Alabama's first sack of the night, forcing a fumble that was recovered by Courtney Upshaw at the Texas 3. Ingram ran the ball three straight times from there—the last a 1-yard touchdown with 2:01 to play, which all but sealed Alabama's victory and championship.

Following Javier Arenas' second interception of the night—and Alabama's fourth of the game—Richardson added a 2-yard scoring run to reach the final margin. All that was left from that point was the celebration, and a time to reflect for a Crimson Tide senior class that had finally and unquestionably helped restore the Alabama program to the top of the college football heap.

"It's been a long process," linebacker Cory Reamer said. "It's been five long years. We've been up, and we've been down. I never would have imagined we'd have had this opportunity to get this victory tonight and be in this position. We appreciate every bit of it. This coaching staff has done a great job and the players have really bought into what we were trying to do as a team. I've never been around a group of guys like this. We jelled from the beginning and we knew that this was something special that we were going to do." ●

No. 1 Alabama vs. No. 2 Texas

	1	2	3	4	Final
Texas	6	0	7	8	21
Record: 13–1					
Alabama	0	24	0	13	37
Record: 14–0					

(above) Greg McElroy, who still hasn't lost a game as a starting quarterback since the eighth grade, was as solid as ever in his decision-making at the helm of the Tide offense. (opposite) Jordan Shipley, who had 10 catches for 122 yards and two touchdowns, did his best to bring his team back, but Alabama's team balance was too much for him or Texas to overcome.

THE HEISMAN MEMORIAL TROPHY

AWARDED ANNUALLY TO THE OUTSTANDING COLLEGE
FOOTBALL PLAYER IN THE UNITED STATES BY THE
HEISMAN TROPHY TRUST

Ingram Makes History with Heisman

The roll call of great Alabama football players is a lengthy one, with nearly 100 first-team All-Americans, numerous NFL stars, and more than a dozen members of the College Football Hall of Fame. Until 2009, however, no Alabama football player had ever been able to call himself a Heisman Trophy winner. The Crimson Tide had had some close calls in the past—Harry Gilmer twice finished in the Top 5 in the 1940s, and David Palmer finished third in 1993, but until sophomore running back Mark Ingram grasped the bronze trophy on the night of December 12, 2009, no Alabama player had ever won the award.

Ingram wept openly at the podium, making his one of the most memorable Heisman speeches of all time. "I'm a little overwhelmed right now," he said. "I'm just so excited to bring Alabama their first Heisman winner."

For Ingram, winning the Heisman Trophy was about family, including father Mark Sr., a longtime NFL standout with whom he maintains a strong relationship despite the older Ingram's well-publicized legal troubles. There's also grandfather Arthur Johnson, a former Canadian Football League star, who loads Ingram's extended family in the car every Alabama game weekend and makes the nearly 900-mile trek from Flint, Michigan to Tuscaloosa, or wherever else the Crimson Tide is playing at the time.

But it is mother Shonda Ingram who has been her son's rock. Ingram said he broke down on the dais after making eye contact with his mother. "When (the Heisman committee chairman) started reading that letter, my heart started beating, and I could feel it beating real fast," he said. "When he called my name I was excited, then I saw my mom crying and it kind of made me break down, too."

The Flint native rushed for a school-record 1,658 yards to with 17 touchdowns in 2009, but mere statistics do not tell the story of Ingram's season. He came up big in the biggest games, bookending his year with 150 yards and two touchdowns in the season-opening win against Virginia Tech and 113 yards and three touchdowns in the Southeastern Conference Championship Game against Florida.

Ingram had nine 100-plus-yard games in all including 116 yards and two scores to earn Offensive Most Valuable Player honors in the BCS National Championship Game. But it was on October 17 against South Carolina that Ingram's Heisman campaign seriously began to take flight. On a night when Alabama's offense struggled for consistency, Ingram carried the load with 246 yards (the third-best total in school history) on 24 carries. Most significant was a fourth-quarter scoring drive on which the 5-foot-10, 212-pound slasher carried the ball six straight times, including the final four yards for the game-clinching touchdown in a 20–6 victory.

"Mark did as fine a job today as anybody I've ever been around, and that includes (NFL Pro Bowlers Ricky Williams and Ronnie Brown and some really good ones," Alabama coach Nick Saban said at the time. "He was fantastic."

Fantastic—against South Carolina and for the entire 2009 season, Ingram certainly was that. ●

Mark Ingram beams as he holds up Alabama's first Heisman Trophy, which together with the BCS National Championship Coaches' Trophy will symbolize this historic Alabama season.

This Time, Alabama Finishes

Alabama 32, Florida 13 • December 5, 2009 • Atlanta, Georgia

A year after having its championship dreams shattered by a furious Florida comeback in the Georgia Dome, Alabama finished the job in 2009. The second-ranked Crimson Tide dominated the top-ranked Gators from the outset, building a two-score early lead and then holding on as Florida rallied. But this time, Alabama was too much for Florida, pitching a second-half shutout and winning 32–13 to punch its ticket to the BCS Championship Game. The Crimson Tide will be chasing its 13th national championship, but first since 1992, when it takes on Big 12 champion Texas on January 7 at the Rose Bowl in Pasadena, California.

"Everyone had to buy into not to be denied in this game," Alabama coach Nick Saban said. "To be a champion, that's what you had to do. I've never been prouder of a group of players."

That "buying in" began not after the Crimson Tide beat Auburn 26–21 to end the regular season, nor when defending national champion Florida pulled within 12–10 early in the second quarter of the SEC Championship Game. It was forged in the rubble of last year's loss to the Gators, in which Florida scored two

fourth-quarter touchdowns to win 31–20 and send Alabama to the Sugar Bowl, where it lost to Utah and tainted a once-promising season.

Saban has harped on "finishing" since his arrival at Alabama in January 2007, but never more so than in the past offseason. As a group, the Crimson Tide knew it didn't want to feel again like it did when it left the Georgia Dome after last year's loss to the Gators.

"That game burned inside us for a whole year, and I know it burned inside coach Saban," senior running back Roy Upchurch said. "I could tell in his speech right before we came out for the kickoff that this team wanted it…and we were ready."

The SEC championship is Alabama's 22nd in its illustrious history but first since 1999 and only its third since the retirement of legendary coach Paul "Bear" Bryant following the 1982 season. The Crimson Tide has won at least one SEC title in every decade since the league formed in 1933, the only conference team to do so.

Alabama's Heisman Trophy candidate, sophomore running back Mark Ingram, had a nice bounce-back game a week after struggling in a win over Auburn.

Mark Ingram and his Crimson Tide teammates were on a mission to take down the favored Florida Gators in the SEC Championship Game.

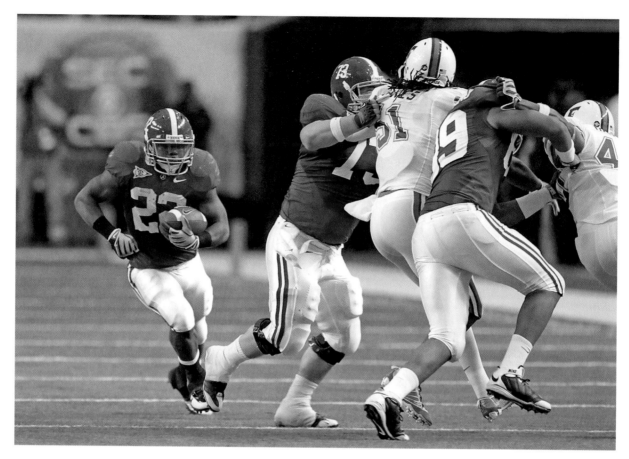

Ingram rushed for 113 yards and three touchdowns, and added 76 yards receiving on two catches to once again place his name firmly in the running for college football's ultimate individual award.

Florida's Tim Tebow, meanwhile, had a miserable night. The 2007 Heisman winner totaled 310 yards rushing and passing, but threw a key interception in the end zone and got the Gators into the paint only once on offense, a year after throwing three touchdown passes against the Crimson Tide.

"It's tough," Tebow said. "You know, it's not how you want to go out. They were just better than us today."

Alabama dominated statistically as well as emotionally, outgaining Florida 490 yards to 335. The Gators entered the game with the country's top-ranked defense and had not allowed anyone to gain more than 357 yards or score more than 20 points all season prior to Alabama's blowout win. The Crimson Tide was well on its way to exceeding those totals by halftime. The Tide rolled up 257 yards of total offense in building a 19–13 lead at the break.

Alabama seized the momentum early, taking the opening kickoff 47 yards in nine plays to set up Leigh Tiffin's 48-yard field goal. The Crimson Tide defense then forced a three-and-out and punt by Florida, and this time, Alabama found the end zone. Alabama drove 76 yards in eight plays, keyed by a 15-yard pass from Greg McElroy to Marquis Maze on third-and-seven. On first-and-goal from the 7, Ingram darted off right tackle for a touchdown and the Crimson Tide led 9–0 with 5:33 left in the first quarter after Tiffin's extra-point attempt hit the right upright.

(above) It was team effort all the way as Alabama's offensive live blew open holes in the Florida defense and gave Ingram plenty of room to operate. (opposite) Try as they might, the Gators simply could not get the immovable object that is Terrence Cody to give any ground.

Florida came right back, however, driving 56 yards in 12 plays for Caleb Sturgis' 48-yard field goal. At the end of a quarter, Alabama's lead had been cut to 9–3.

The two teams then exchanged punts before Alabama got on the board again. This time it was Tiffin from 34 yards away to make it 12–3 after a drive kept alive on an amazing run by McElroy, who tap-danced along the right sideline for a key first down three plays before the field goal.

McElroy ended the game with 239 yards and one touchdown on 12 of 18 passing. In extending his personal streak to 29 consecutive victories as a starting quarterback dating back to high school, the junior from Southlake, Texas, was named the game's Most Valuable Player.

"You leave the field wondering who was the Heisman candidate coming into the game," Tide guard Mike Johnson said. "He played lights out. He plays with such a big heart."

But Florida was far from done after merely a quarter-and-a-half. The Gators answered with a four-play, 70-yard drive, including two long runs by Tebow, which ended on Tebow's 23-yard touchdown pass to David Nelson. With 4:31 left in the first half, Alabama's lead was 12–10.

Alabama's biggest offensive play of the night gave back the momentum to the Crimson Tide. Ingram took a short pass from McElroy and raced 69 yards to the Florida 3. He ran the ball in on the next play to put Alabama back up by two scores.

Florida would drive quickly for Sturgis' 32-yard field goal to make it 19-13 just before the half, and had a chance to take the lead when it received the opening kickoff of the third quarter. But Alabama's defense forced a three-and-out and a punt, and the Tide put the Gators away from there.

Ingram ran three times for a first down, then McElroy

Greg McElroy, who has been solid all season, came of age in the SEC Championship Game with cool leadership and timely passing.

hit Maze for 28 yards to get into Florida territory. A roughing-the-passer call moved the ball to the Florida 17, and McElroy hit tight end Colin Peek—who made a beautiful over-the-shoulder catch in the end zone—for a 17-yard touchdown, and Alabama was back up by two scores with 9:53 left in the third quarter.

Florida had to punt on its next drive, and Alabama proceeded to take the air out of the game. The Crimson Tide one-upped its memorable drive from a week prior, when it moved 79 yards in 15 plays to score the winning touchdown against Auburn. This time, Alabama moved 88 yards in 17 plays and erased the second half of the third quarter. The Tide converted five third downs on the drive, four of them on runs by Ingram. The last of those gave the Crimson Tide third-and-goal on the 1, and Ingram punched the ball in on the next play. A two-point

attempt failed, but with 13:49 remaining in the game, Alabama led by three scores at 32–13.

Ingram did all that despite the lingering effects of a painful hip pointer suffered late in the Auburn game. In the process, he broke Bobby Humphrey's single-season Alabama rushing record (1,471, set in 1986) and has 1,542 yards and an SEC-best 15 touchdowns headed into the BCS title game.

"Mark showed a lot of resolve today," Saban said. "He did practice, but he really wasn't full speed until Thursday. We didn't know how he'd respond. But he went for it today. Played a great game. I'm really proud of the character he showed coming off last week's performance, as well as coming off the injury he had. He showed a lot of mental toughness and grit."

After Ingram's final touchdown, it was up to the

(above) Marquis Maze lunges for extra yards in a performance that included five catches for 96 yards. (opposite) Mark Ingram was the focal point of the Alabama offense with 28 carries, 113 yards, and three touchdowns. Florida had a hard time laying a hand on him because of the Tide's great blocking up front.

Florida's star quarterback Tim Tebow did what he could, but Eryk Anders and the rest of the Alabama defense harassed him all day long.

Alabama defense to make the lead stand up. Florida's last two drives ended with a Javier Arenas interception in the end zone and a dropped fourth-down pass at the Crimson Tide 13.

Alabama's offense killed the game's last 7:28, and McElroy twice took a knee inside the Florida 15 to run off the final seconds. That set off the Crimson Tide's first football championship celebration in a decade, and set up a shot at Alabama's 13th national championship.

"If you want to be a champion, you have to have a team of champions," McElroy said. "This team came out and proved itself a champion."

Still, the Crimson Tide left the field knowing that its mission was not yet accomplished. The Texas Longhorns, a team Alabama is 0–7–1 against all-time, awaits the Tide at the Rose Bowl. That stadium has been

the site of many past Alabama memorable moments, including national championships won following the 1925, 1926, and 1934 seasons.

"We're happy about this (SEC) championship, but we all want to accomplish bigger things," Ingram said.

For the first time in 17 years, Alabama will get its shot to take home college football's ultimate prize. ●

No. 2 Alabama vs. No. 1 Florida

	1	2	3	4	Final
Florida	3	10	0	0	13
Record: 12–1					
Alabama	9	10	7	6	32
Record: 13–0					

(above) Leigh Tiffin and Brain Selman celebrate up close and personal as the Tide rolled early and dominated most of the game. (opposite) On the rare occasion when quarterback Tim Tebow did have time to pass, defensive backs like Kareem Jackson stepped up to make plays and keep Florida frustrated.

Déjà Vu, Georgia Dome Style

Alabama 34, Virginia Tech 24 • September 5, 2009 • Atlanta, Georgia

For the second straight time, Alabama started its season with a nationally televised showdown, facing a top 10 team in Atlanta's Georgia Dome. But this time, the Crimson Tide wasn't sneaking up on anyone. A year after No. 24 Alabama crushed ninth-ranked Clemson 34–10, expectations were much higher for the Crimson Tide, which entered the 2009 season ranked No. 5 in the country. Its opponent, No. 7 Virginia Tech, held the esteem of most everyone in the college football world, including Alabama coach Nick Saban.

"We are playing a very, very good team," Saban said in his Monday press conference to kick off game week. "Virginia Tech is an outstanding football team. They have been an outstanding team, they know how to win.

The meeting was the first between Alabama and Virginia Tech since the 1998 Music City Bowl in Nashville, which the Hokies won in a rout, 34–7. A capacity crowd of 74,954 packed into the Georgia Dome for the 2009 game, which began with Alabama's defense forcing Virginia Tech to go three-and-out. But Alabama's offense stalled out itself after one first down, and the Crimson Tide settled for Leigh Tiffin's 49-yard field goal and a 3–0 lead.

Alabama forced another three-and-out on the Hokies' next possession, which led to another field goal, this one from 34 yards away, to give the Tide a 6–0 lead. That advantage was short-lived as Virginia Tech's Dyrell Roberts gathered in the ensuing kickoff and burst up the left side for a 98-yard touchdown and a 7–6 Hokies lead.

Alabama continued to struggle on offense, but a Hokies fumble led to a third Tiffin field goal, enough for the Tide to reclaim the lead at 9–7. The Hokies added a field goal of their own after picking off a Greg McElroy pass and the score was 10–9 in Tech's favor.

McElroy finally overcame his poor debut as starting quarterback on Alabama's next possession, hitting Julio Jones for gains of 10 and 16 yards. Running back Roy Upchurch raced into the end zone from 19 yards out to put the Tide up 16–10 with 3:09 left in the half.

Alabama was flagged for three penalties on Virginia Tech's next possession—which was highlighted by running back Ryan Williams' 43-yard pass reception and 1-yard touchdown run—and ended up trailing 17–16 at the end of two quarters. "We lost our poise there in the two-minute situation on defense and gave them a touchdown basically on

It took three tries, but the Crimson Tide finally earned the program's 800th victory. Roy Upchurch carried only seven times but made his touches count, going for 90 yards and a score.

penalties and a busted coverage," Saban said at the half."

The score remained 17–16 into the fourth quarter. The Crimson Tide finally took charge after a 14-yard Javier Arenas punt return gave Alabama the ball on its own 46. McElroy went deep on the first play, connecting with Marquis Maze for 48 yards to the Virginia Tech 6. Mark Ingram raced into the end zone for the touchdown on the next play, then McElroy hit Colin Peek for two points and a 24–17 Bama lead. Virginia Tech fumbled the ensuing kickoff, which the Tide converted into a Tiffin field goal and a 27–17 margin.

Virginia Tech wasn't quite done, however, as a long kickoff return and a facemask penalty led to a quick Ryan Williams 32-yard touchdown run with 9:22 remaining, cutting Alabama's lead to three. Ingram was the star of Alabama's next possession, running for 39 yards on first down and getting into the end zone after racing 18 yards with a short toss from McElroy. That gave Alabama a 34–24 lead with just over six minutes left in the game.

Any hopes of a Virginia Tech comeback were dashed when Alabama's defense ended the Hokies' last two possessions with sacks. All told, the Crimson Tide allowed just 155 yards in the game, while piling up 498.

Ingram proved he could carry the load for the departed Glen Coffee, totaling 150 yards on 26 carries, with one touchdown each rushing and receiving. McElroy overcame a rough start to finish 15-for-30 for 230 yards and one touchdown, with one interception.

It wasn't always pretty, but Alabama came away from its second straight Atlanta opener with a 1–0 record and an impressive victory against a highly ranked team. ●

No. 5 Alabama vs. No. 7 Virginia Tech

	1	2	3	4	Final
Alabama	9	7	0	18	34
Record: 1–0					
Virginia Tech	7	10	0	7	24
Record: 0–1					

Darius Hanks lays out for a 35-yard grab from Greg McElroy. Statistically, the game was one of Hanks' best of the year as he and the receiving corps helped McElroy notch 230 passing yards.

Home, and Cooking

Alabama 40, Florida International 14 • September 12, 2009 • Tuscaloosa, Alabama

I f Alabama's season-opening game against Virginia Tech was played under a blinding national spotlight, things were much more subdued for the Crimson Tide's home opener at Bryant-Denny Stadium. The opponent was Florida International, one of the more obscure programs in the NCAA's Football Bowl Subdivision. The teams had met only once previously, with the Crimson Tide claiming a 38–3 win in 2006.

The 2009 Golden Panthers team was a bit more competitive than it had been three years earlier and showed it in taking a one-point lead in the first half. But Alabama, which had moved up to No. 4 in the national rankings following Oklahoma's loss to BYU, used a balanced offensive attack to steamroll through the second half and come away with a 40–14 victory and a 2–0 record.

Alabama rushed for 275 yards and passed for 241, getting a near-flawless performance from quarterback Greg McElroy. The junior completed 18 of 24 passes, with a touchdown and an interception. He did most of that without star receiver Julio Jones, who sustained a bruised knee in the first half and did not return. Also at less-than-100-percent were No. 1 running back Mark Ingram (illness) and all-purpose back Roy Upchurch (ankle). That left plenty of opportunities for younger players, including freshman running back Trent Richardson, who rushed for 119 yards and two touchdowns. Alabama also got a career-high 100 yards receiving from senior Mike McCoy.

The Crimson Tide defense also did its part, holding FIU to 214 yards of total offense, including 1 net rushing yard on 26 attempts. Linebacker Rolando McClain led the way with 10 tackles, while Marcell Dareus had two sacks and Mark Barron picked up his first career interception.

Despite the dominant margin of victory and overwhelming statistical edge, Alabama coach Nick Saban was less than pleased with his team's overall performance. "I really wasn't happy with the energy and enthusiasm our team came out and played with in the first half," Saban said. "The focus in games like this is to improve. FIU's players played well in the game, they played hard. I don't think our guys came out with the kind of energy, enthusiasm and intensity that we need to set the tone, and we allowed them to stay in the game

With key players like Julio Jones and Mark Ingram out of action against Florida International, other players got the chance to shine under the bright home lights. Freshman back Trent Richardson had his best day of the season, carrying for 118 yards and two touchdowns.

with some mistakes that we made and some things that we didn't do correctly."

Alabama scored the first two times it had the ball to take a 10–0 lead. Leigh Tiffin connected on a 23-yard field goal to make it 3–0, then the Crimson Tide defense forced a punt. On Alabama's second possession, McElroy found McCoy open for a 24-yard touchdown and a two-score lead.

But as Virginia Tech had done the week before, Florida International first cracked the scoreboard thanks to its special teams. T.Y. Hilton gathered in Tiffin's kickoff and raced 96 yards for a touchdown, the second kickoff return for a touchdown the Crimson Tide had allowed in as many weeks.

Alabama answered with Tiffin's 29-yard field goal to make it 13–7, but FIU was able to get the best of the Crimson Tide's defense for the only time all day on its ensuing drive. The Golden Panthers drove 60 yards in eight plays, culminating in Paul McCall's 9-yard touchdown pass to Greg Ellingson to make it FIU 14, Alabama 13 with 10:29 left in the first half.

Alabama retook the lead with a methodical scoring drive, marching 69 yards in five plays for a touchdown. McElroy hit McCoy for 35 yards on the first play, and Ingram scored from the 2 to make it 20–14, a score that would stand up until the half.

The Crimson Tide thoroughly dominated the second half, scoring touchdowns on three of four possessions at one stretch and holding FIU to five first downs in the last two quarters. Those scores were a 9-yard run by

Richardson (Alabama missed a two-point conversion attempt), a 35-yard run by Richardson, and a 42-yard run by Terry Grant.

With the Hokies and Golden Panthers out of the way, that left only a home game with North Texas before the Crimson Tide's Southeastern Conference schedule began. ●

No. 4 Alabama vs. Florida International

	1	2	3	4	Final
Fla. International Record: 0–1	7	7	0	0	14
Alabama Record: 2–0	10	10	6	14	40

(above) The Golden Panthers offense must have felt caged in after their date with the Alabama defense. The Florida International offense attempted 26 rushes but accumulated only one yard. (opposite) McElroy had an efficient outing even without his favorite target, Julio Jones, completing all but six of his passes for 241 yards and a first quarter touchdown.

It's Not Easy Being (Mean) Green

Alabama 53, North Texas 7 • September 19, 2009 • Tuscaloosa, Alabama

Alabama's first snap was a near-disaster, but it was hard to quibble with much of anything else in the Crimson Tide's 53–7 victory over North Texas. The Crimson Tide fumbled the ball away on the first play of the game, but scored on six straight possessions and nine of 11 overall in its most dominant performance of the season. Alabama, No. 4 in the national rankings for the second straight week, outgained North Texas 523 yards to 187 to improve to 3–0 on the year headed into SEC play.

Alabama played without star wide receiver Julio Jones (knee) and running back Roy Upchurch (ankle), though starting running back Mark Ingram returned at full strength after a bout with the flu. Sixty-five players saw action in the game, with 11 different receivers catching passes and four different backs rushing for touchdowns.

"Even though the first play wasn't good, I felt like we dominated the line of scrimmage and the game for probably the first time in the beginning of a game all year," Alabama coach Nick Saban said. "We got to play a lot of players and the experience will be very valuable

for them down the road relative to our depth. Obviously, when we put some two's in one defense, they made a couple big plays and made some mental errors, but they'll learn from those things and we'll get better and that's the kind of game experience we need."

After quarterback Greg McElroy fumbled deep in Alabama territory on the game's first play, the Crimson Tide defense forced the Mean Green to go three-and-out. That set off a scoring barrage for Alabama, which led 30–0 at halftime and 44–0 at one point in the third quarter.

Alabama drove 95 yards for its first touchdown, a 2-yard bootleg scramble by McElroy. The Crimson Tide quarterback threw 34 yards to Marquis Maze to make it 14-0 after one quarter.

Trent Richardson's 1-yard touchdown run—the third in two games for the freshman—made it 21–0, then McElroy hooked up with Ingram on a 29-yard touchdown pass for a 27–0 lead after the extra point failed. Leigh Tiffin rebounded from that miss to connect on a 35-yard field goal on the last play of the half to make it 30–0.

Javier Arenas' 36-yard punt return set Alabama up for a touchdown in the third quarter, with Ingram's 5-yard run

Nicknamed after Hall-of-Fame defensive tackle Mean Joe Greene, the North Texas defense lived up to its billing for one play, forcing a fumble on Alabama's first play from scrimmage. The rest of the game was ugly for the Mean Green: Greg McElroy threw just two incomplete passes and the rushing attack amassed 260 yards.

putting the Tide up 37–0. The Crimson Tide actually had to punt on its next possession, but got Terry Grant's 1-yard run late in the third quarter to make it 44–0.

North Texas finally got on the board near the end of the quarter, a 34-yard touchdown pass from Nathan Tune to Lance Dunbar. Alabama closed the game out with a pair of fourth-quarter scores behind back-up quarterback Star Jackson, a 20-yard Tiffin field goal and a 9-yard Grant run.

"Today we came out and we wanted to start early," Alabama linebacker Dont'a Hightower said. "We haven't been doing it the past couple games so we had to this game. We're not just a 'finish' team, we're a 'start and finish' team. We came out with the right mentality and right focus and we were obviously communicating very well. I think that was the key for us today."

Ingram ended the day with 91 rushing yards and a touchdown on eight carries , plus 38 receiving yards and another score on three catches. Richardson added 87 yards and a touchdown, while Grant had 79 yards and two scores as part of Alabama's 260-yard day on the ground. McElroy was near-perfect again, going 13-for-15 for 176 yards and two scores. Jackson, in his first extended action, went 9-for-13 for 87 yards through the air.

The win over North Texas completed the pre-conference schedule for the Crimson Tide. The season was set to begin the following week against Arkansas, the first of seven games in eight weeks against SEC opposition. ●

No. 4 Alabama vs. North Texas

	1	2	3	4	Final
North Texas	0	0	7	0	7
Record: 1–2					
Alabama	14	16	14	9	53
Record: 3–0					

Mark Ingram carried only eight times but still managed 91 yards and a score for an impressive average of over 11 yards per carry.

Tide's McElroy Nothing but a Winner

The streak is at 29 and counting for Greg McElroy. That's how many consecutive victories McElroy has as a starting quarterback. It's also how many games he's started at quarterback since the beginning of his senior year of high school.

McElroy won all 16 games his senior year at Southlake (Texas) Carroll High School, leading the Dragons to the 2005 state championship in Class 5A, Texas' biggest classification. After a three-year break sitting behind John Parker Wilson, he's won his first 13 games leading the Alabama offense.

So it's safe to say you can call McElroy a "winner." But his teammates and coaches have also noticed another quality in him. "He's just a great leader," wide receiver Darius Hanks said. "He's a people's person."

While McElroy has not put up the massive statistics of some previous Alabama quarterbacks, he has done what most championship-caliber signal-callers have done—avoid the killer mistake. He's also shown the patience to wait for the right moment to make a big play, as he did with late touchdown passes to help seal victories over Virginia Tech, Arkansas, and Mississippi State.

Biding his time is a skill McElroy first learned in high school, when he sat behind future Missouri standout Chase Daniel until his senior season. He waited his turn again at Alabama, finally taking over after two seasons of serving as Wilson's primary back-up.

"I've had a chance to study different types of quarterbacks such as John Parker and Chase and guys I've been around and backed up," McElroy said. "I think that's really added a different dimension to my game.

"Before my senior year, I actually had double-digit scholarship offers, Texas Tech, North Carolina, a lot of schools. I was very fortunate that I was able to get noticed because of Chase. When they would come to spring practice, they would recruit him but they would go away asking about me. Obviously, going to camps helped me a lot in getting noticed. I probably wouldn't be here if Chase wasn't the quarterback ahead of me."

When Wilson moved on, McElroy was not assured a starting job (players never are in Saban's system). He would have to beat out redshirt freshman Star Jackson—one of the stars of the Crimson Tide's 2008 recruiting class—and sophomore walk-on Thomas Darrah in the spring to win the job.

Waiting for his chance to shine has been the story of Greg McElroy's career: he sat behind Chase Daniel in high school then backed up John Parker Wilson at Alabama. His patience has paid off, and he's made the most of his opportunities—he has not lost a game as starter, dating back to his days at Texas' Southlake Carroll High School.

His rushing numbers are distorted by sacks, but McElroy is not an immobile pocket passer. He carried for 100 total yards during the regular season and added a touchdown.

It turned out to be not much of a competition, as McElroy had secured the job by the second scrimmage of the spring. He's maintained that stranglehold ever since, as Jackson and Darrah have appeared on the field only in blowouts.

"Greg has stood out a lot to me," running back Roy Upchurch said. "He went, in my opinion, from just a regular quarterback to a quarterback that will wow you. I think he's more of a spread-it-around type of quarterback. He'll get it to everybody and get it out his hands real fast. He's really opened my eyes this year."

McElroy has quickly become among the most popular players on the Alabama roster, which is true of any winning quarterback. As the old football saw goes, quarterbacks get far too much credit when a team wins, and far too much blame when they lose. McElroy hasn't yet experienced the second half of that maxim, and probably isn't in any hurry to find out how it feels. He's chosen to lean on his more-experienced teammates at times, rather than try to carry the Crimson Tide by himself.

"I don't think it's any single individual's team," McElroy said. "I think we've got a good group of guys who take ownership and work hard. I don't think it can be any one person's team, it's a collective effort and that's the way we're going to get the most out of this team."

Aside from his experience in winning programs before taking over the starting job, McElroy also possesses all the other attributes needed to be a successful quarterback. He's got prototypical size (6-foot-3, 220 pounds) and a strong, accurate throwing arm. But what might set him apart is his intelligence, which is off-the-charts even for the cerebral position of quarterback. McElroy graduated in three years with a degree in business marketing and carried a 3.85 grade point average to earn magna cum laude honors.

"He is very smart, a very bright guy and has a good understanding of the offense," Alabama coach Nick Saban said. "Players really like him. He has a lot of positive leadership qualities and he does affect other people. He's very instinctive and he makes good choices and decisions at his position."

McElroy also possesses the hunger that burns in most big-time athletes. For all his success this year and in previous seasons, he still sees his—and his team's—mission as far from finished. He's hoping that day of culmination comes for himself and the Crimson Tide on January 7 in Pasadena.

"You know the day you play your best football should be the last game of every year," McElroy said. "I think we're continually improving. I think everybody is trying to improve personally, individually and obviously collectively we're trying to accomplish all of our goals. Our best football is out there. When we come back and look at the film on Mondays there are things that we did wrong. That's natural and you're never going play a perfect game."

Maybe not, but you can have a perfect record. Greg McElroy is living proof of that. ●

Since nothing is guaranteed with Coach Saban, McElroy had to come in and work for the starting job in 2009. He may not be the perfect NFL quarterback prospect but he has something far more important—a perfect record.

A Big Win, but a Big Loss

Alabama 35, Arkansas 7 • September 26, 2009 • Tuscaloosa, Alabama

The annual game with Arkansas has generally been an excellent gauge for how good a team Alabama has. Coming very early in the season (and often as the first Southeastern Conference game), the annual match-up with the Razorbacks has many times served as either a tone-setter or a season-killer for the Crimson Tide.

Alabama blasted Arkansas 49–14 in Fayetteville in 2008, one of its big early victories on the way to an SEC West Division championship. But Bobby Petrino's Razorbacks were a year older and a year wiser this time around, and sported one of the top newcomers in the conference in quarterback Ryan Mallett, a Michigan transfer. The rifle-armed Mallett had blistered Georgia for 408 yards and five touchdowns the previous week, though Arkansas lost that game 52–41. Still, the Razorbacks had coach Nick Saban's full attention heading into game week.

"Bobby Petrino has always been one of the best offensive coaches, wherever he has been or whatever level," Saban said the Monday before the game. "They have a great passing game; a very good system.... This is a really good football team, especially an outstanding offensive team, but a really good team overall and it's going to be very challenging for us. It's a little different than what we have played against to this point, so there are a lot of challenges here and we'll see how we respond to it."

Alabama had moved up one more notch in the national rankings to No. 3 following Southern Cal's shocking loss to Washington. The Crimson Tide was also getting a boost from the return of two injured standouts, starting wide receiver Julio Jones and all-purpose back Roy Upchurch, who had missed the North Texas game with knee and ankle injuries, respectively.

The Arkansas game turned out to be not terribly competitive, as Alabama used big plays to overcome a slow start offensive and come away with a 35–7 victory on a rainy day in Bryant-Denny Stadium. The two teams were scoreless through one quarter, but the Crimson Tide broke loose for a pair of long scoring plays in the second period.

It began with a memorable run by freshman Trent Richardson, who broke at least five tackles on his way to a

Hanks hauls in one of McElroy's 17 completions. The quarterback finished with a season-high 291 yards and three touchdowns in a torching of the Razorback secondary.

52-yard touchdown and a 7–0 Alabama lead. The Crimson Tide defense then forced a punt, and Javier Arenas returned the ball to midfield to set up the next big play.

On the Crimson Tide's first play from scrimmage, Mark Ingram took a snap out of the Wildcat formation and handed to receiver Marquis Maze, who pitched the ball back to Greg McElroy. The Alabama quarterback found a wide-open Jones, who gathered in the ball and bounded into the end zone for his first touchdown of the season and a 14–0 Crimson Tide lead.

Arkansas' offense finally struck in the third quarter, driving 55 yards in five plays for a touchdown on Mallett's 18-yard pass to Greg Childs, which made it 14–7. But just as quickly, Alabama hit another big play to take the wind out of the Razorback's sails, this time for good. McElroy threw deep on first down, finding Maze behind the defense for an 80-yard touchdown and a 21–7 lead. The Razorbacks never again made it into the red zone, and Alabama tacked on two Ingram touchdowns—a 14-yard reception and a 2-yard run—to win going away.

McElroy had his third straight big day passing, going 17-for-24 for 291 yards and three touchdowns, with no interceptions. The Crimson Tide defense sacked Mallett three times, including twice on corner blitzes by Arenas.

Mallett, who led the country in passing efficiency coming in, was just 12-for-35 for 160 yards with a touchdown and an interception. The Razorbacks ended the day with 254 yards of total offense, and went 2-for-14 on third down.

Nevertheless, the enthusiasm for the decisive victory was tempered somewhat by a major injury in the first quarter. Linebacker Dont'a Hightower, a freshman All-American in 2008 and one of the stalwarts of the Crimson Tide's outstanding defense, sustained torn knee

Julio Jones scampers into the end zone on his 50-yard touchdown strike from Greg McElroy. Nine different players caught passes for the Crimson Tide, with no player having more than three grabs.

ligaments when he was hit on a low (but legal) block by Arkansas lineman Mitch Petrus.

The sophomore underwent surgery the following week, but is on track to return in time for spring practice in 2010. Still, as a starting inside linebacker, special teams standout, and occasional pass-rushing defensive end who had totaled 16 tackles, four tackles for loss, and a sack in little more than three games in 2009, Hightower would be difficult to replace.

"I don't know that you can replace a guy that does all the things that he did," Saban said.

The Tide soldiered on against Arkansas by shifting several linebackers around. Cory Reamer moved inside to Hightower's Will (weak inside) linebacker position from Sam (strong outside) linebacker, while Eryk Anders switched from Jack (weak outside) linebacker to Sam. Sophomore Courtney Upshaw checked in at Jack. In later weeks, freshman Nico Johnson would take over at Will, with Reamer mov-

ing back to Sam and Anders back to Jack.

But just as important as the on-field production was the psychological effect of the Crimson Tide's defense being robbed of one of its leaders. Hightower's injury had a deep impact on junior Rolando McClain, his fellow starting inside linebacker and close friend.

"He's not just my teammate, he's like a little brother to me," McClain said the following week. "We've been like that since he got here. When he went out, it was like a part of me went out."

Alabama would have to regroup in a hurry, however, as its first true road game of the season was coming up the next week at Kentucky. ●

No. 3 Alabama vs. Arkansas

	1	2	3	4	Final
Arkansas	0	0	7	0	7
Record: 1–2, 0–2 SEC					
Alabama	0	14	14	7	35
Record: 4–0, 1–0 SEC					

(above) Javier Arenas, who had two sacks in the game, and the 'Bama defense harassed a potent Razorback offense all day long. (opposite) Roy Upchurch searches for daylight with blockers in front of him. Upchurch finished without a carry but caught three passes out of the backfield for 30 yards.

Rolling through the Bluegrass

Alabama 38, Kentucky 20 • October 3, 2009 • Lexington, Kentucky

Alabama had history on its side heading into its October 3 game at Kentucky. After all, the Crimson Tide had lost to the Wildcats just twice in its history and only once since 1922. And it was off to a 4–0 start in 2009, with Kentucky coming off a 41–7 home loss to Florida.

Third-ranked Alabama had dominated its last 15 quarters of play, having rallied for a season-opening win against Virginia Tech and then cruising past Florida International, North Texas, and Arkansas in succession. The 35–7 win over the Razorbacks had been perhaps the Crimson Tide's best performance of the season, and the Alabama players were beginning to smell a championship run.

"It's safe to say that the momentum is building, but I think it's excitement more than anything," cornerback Javier Arenas said. "I think there is a lot of room for improvement, as it is always, but it did let us know where we're at, and what we're capable of. It's not a sign of relaxing and chilling out because we're good. It's time to realize how good we could be and let's get to that level. Let's minus the mistakes and get to where we should be."

The Kentucky game did present a few concerns, however. In running back/kick returner Derrick Locke and wide receiver/quarterback Randall Cobb, the Wildcats possessed two of the better playmakers in the Southeastern Conference. Also of note was that this would be Alabama's first true road game of the season. The Crimson Tide had played Virginia Tech at a neutral site—Atlanta—to open the schedule, but had yet to venture into a hostile road environment.

"It's not like playing at home," coach Nick Saban said. "So this will be a challenge for us. All SEC games are difficult; playing on the road in an SEC game is always difficult. Kentucky has a very good program…so this is going to be a challenging game for us in all phases of the game. This is probably the best team we have played so far in terms of just running the ball…but I am sure we'll get it in this game and that'll be a challenge for our players as well."

Unlike the previous week against Arkansas, Alabama got off to fast start against the Wildcats. Javier Arenas returned the opening kickoff 60 yards to the Kentucky 37, and the Crimson Tide needed just

Kentucky kept the game within striking range for much of the first half, but the Crimson Tide ended any hopes for an upset with Courtney Upshaw's fumble return for a touchdown with just 21 seconds left in the second quarter.

three plays to reach the end zone.

Kentucky was flagged for roughing-the-passer on first down, moving the ball to the 22. Mark Ingram ran six yards on the next play, then bolted through the Wildcats defense for a 17-yard touchdown to make it 7–0 Alabama just 57 seconds into the game.

The Tide offense struggled for most of the rest of the half, however, and Kentucky pulled within 7–6 on two Lones Seiber field goals. The Wildcats pinned Alabama at its own 3 on a punt with 7:30 left in the half, and the Crimson Tide narrowly avoided disaster.

Freshman running back Trent Richardson took a handoff and was hit in the end zone, but was able to escape a safety by inching the ball across the goal-line just before hitting the turf. Ingram, who was on the sideline while his substitute was in the game, watched in horror.

"I thought it was a safety, personally," Ingram said.

But a replay review confirmed that it wasn't, and games and seasons can turn on such a play. The Crimson Tide took advantage of its good fortune, embarking on a 97-yard drive—which featured three third-down conversion passes—that ended on Greg McElroy's 3-yard TD pass to Colin Peek, giving Alabama a 14–6 lead with 40 seconds left in the half.

Moments later, Alabama linebacker Rolando McClain jarred the ball loose from Locke on a short pass. Courtney Upshaw, making his first start of the year following the season-ending injury to Dont'a Hightower, plucked the ball out of the air and rambled 45 yards for a touchdown—Alabama's second in 19 seconds—and a 21–6 halftime advantage for the Crimson Tide.

"It was huge," McElroy said. "We were just happy with the one touchdown. I mean you get a two-touchdown swing in our favor at the end of a half, it kills all the momentum for them and leans all in our favor."

Alabama forced two more turnovers in the third

(above) The Crimson Wall helped keep the Wildcats down all game long. (opposite) Colin Peek led the Alabama receiving corps against Kentucky. The senior tight end hauled in six balls for 65 yards and a score in the best game of his career.

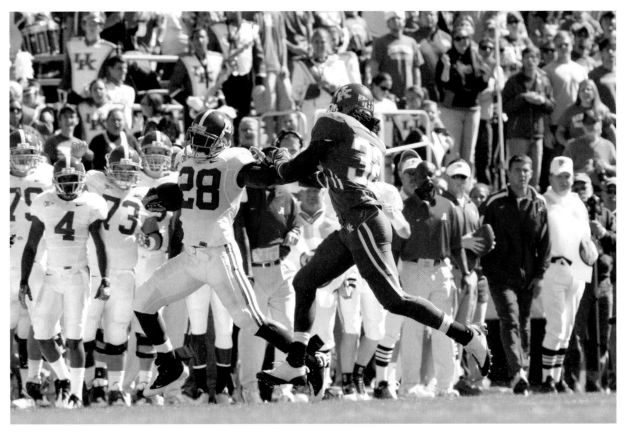

quarter to build a 31–6 advantage. McClain came up with the first pick, leading to Mark Ingram's 32-yard TD run. McClain then deflected another pass into the hands of Eryk Anders—meaning McClain was responsible for three consecutive turnovers—to set up Leigh Tiffin's 36-yard field goal.

Kentucky finally got into the end zone late in the quarter on Mike Hartline's 45-yard touchdown pass to Cobb, but Alabama answered with McElroy's 7-yard scoring toss to Darius Hanks to make it 38–13. The Wildcats closed out the scoring on Alfonso Smith's 2-yard run early in the fourth quarter, but the Crimson Tide defense shut things down from there, and Alabama cruised to the 18-point victory.

McClain ended the game with 12 tackles, a forced fumble, an interception, and a quarterback hurry, earning both SEC and national defensive player of the week honors

for his performance. Ingram chipped in 140 yards (his career-best to that point) and two touchdowns, while McElroy was 15-for-26 with two touchdown passes.

Alabama's point total put it over 30 for the fifth consecutive game, the first time it had done so to start a season since 1922 and the first time it had done so at any point since 1979. The Crimson Tide won the national championship that latter year, and appeared poised to make a run at another in 2009 following its convincing road win at Kentucky. ●

No. 3 Alabama at Kentucky

	1	2	3	4	Final
Alabama	7	14	17	0	38
Record: 5–0, 2–0 SEC					
Kentucky	6	0	7	7	20
Record: 2–2, 0–2 SEC					

(above) The electric Javier Arenas streaks down the sideline. The return specialist also had a great game defensively, picking up a season-high eight tackles. (opposite) Cool and efficient yet again, McElroy threw for 148 yards and two scores. More importantly, he finished again without an interception.

Defense Carries the Day

Alabama 22, Mississippi 3 • October 10, 2009 • Oxford, Mississippi

If you didn't know any better, you'd have thought Mississippi was the team coming off a 12–2 season and a Southeastern Conference West Division championship with the way the Rebels were being talked up during the off-season. Sure, Ole Miss had finished as one of the hotter teams in the country in 2008, winning its last five regular-season games and crushing Texas Tech in the Cotton Bowl. The Rebels had also been the only team to beat national champion Florida and returned a boatload of talent, including quarterback Jevan Snead, running back Dexter McCluster, defensive end Greg Hardy, and wide receiver Shay Hodge.

What many didn't remember, however, is that the Rebels' last loss had come to none other than Alabama, a 24–20 Crimson Tide win in Tuscaloosa. In fact, Alabama had beaten Ole Miss five straight times and in 45 of 57 meetings all-time headed into the October 10 meeting at Vaught-Hemingway Stadium in Oxford, Mississippi.

And while Alabama cruised into the game 5–0 and ranked No. 3 in the country, cracks had already started to appear for coach Houston Nutt's Rebels. Snead was off to a rocky start statistically, and Ole Miss had been beaten two weeks prior, a 16–10 loss at South Carolina that dropped the Rebels out of the national Top 10. But given the talent on the opposing sideline and the big-game atmosphere sure to greet them in Oxford (many in the Ole Miss community billed this as the Rebels' biggest on-campus game in 40 years), Alabama coach Nick Saban was taking nothing for granted.

"[Mississippi] is probably the best team we have played to this point, all the way around," Saban said. "They have a lot of experience, a lot of good players, and a very good defensive team. Houston Nutt does a great job coaching any team that he has coached and we have had some great games in the past.... I think our team needs to be focused on what we need to do to improve and play the kind of winning football it's going to take on the road to beat a good football team like this."

And play winning football is what Alabama did. What had been billed as one of the SEC "games of the year" by many national pundits turned out to be merely business as usual for the Crimson Tide.

Alabama struggled offensively, getting into the end

Although it was a fairly quiet day for the Alabama passing game—especially compared to Leigh Tiffin's kicking and Mark Ingram's running—Colin Peek caught three passes against Ole Miss.

Hungry to get after Ole Miss—one of the country's most-hyped teams entering the 2009 season—the Alabama defense was more than ready to punish the Rebels' offense. Jevan Snead was hit early and often while being forced into throwing four interceptions. Cory Reamer had a great day for the Crimson Tide, adding a blocked punt and a fumble recovery to this hit on the quarterback.

zone just once all day. But the Crimson Tide defense saved the day, holding Ole Miss to 197 yards of total offense and forcing five turnovers on the way to a 22–3 victory at Vaught-Hemingway Stadium.

The Crimson Tide punted on its first two possessions of the game before finally cracking the scoreboard late in the first quarter. A long drive bogged down inside the Ole Miss 5, prompting Saban to call on Leigh Tiffin to kick a 25-yard field goal, his first of five 3-pointers on the day.

Alabama led 3–0 after one quarter, but defense and special teams led to two more field goals in the second quarter. Javier Arenas intercepted Snead at the Ole Miss 26 to set up Tiffin's 21-yarder, while Cory Reamer's blocked punt put the Tide in position for a 22-yarder to make it 9–0.

After petering out three times inside the Ole Miss 10, the Crimson Tide offense at long last reached the end zone just before halftime, using a fourth-and-1 gamble to get there. From the Ole Miss 36, Mark Ingram took a short-side pitch around left end and was gone for the touchdown, putting Alabama up 16–0 at the half.

Contrary to the offensive struggles, Alabama's defense completely shut down the Rebels in the first half. Snead was 2-for-12 with two interceptions and Ole Miss managed just five rushing yards in the first two quarters. "That was as fine a defensive performance in the first half as I've been around," Saban said.

The second half was a slow march to victory for the Crimson Tide, though the Rebels did finally get on the board on Joshua Shene's 25-yard field goal in the third quarter. Alabama continued to harass Snead, intercepting him twice more and forcing a fifth Ole Miss turnover on a punt return.

"You could tell by some of the passes he was throwing," Arenas said. "We know what type of quarterback he is, and we know what he is capable of. We were trying to get some hits on him and get him rattled. We could tell the difference in passing decision-making."

Alabama's second-half points came on two more Tiffin field goals, from 21 yards in the third quarter and 31 yards in the fourth (Tiffin would be named SEC Special Teams Player of the Week for his five-field-goal effort). The Crimson Tide outgained the Rebels 354 yards to 197 in the game, including 200 to 57 on the ground.

Ingram continued to make his case as a Heisman Trophy candidate, with 172 yards and a touchdown on 28 carries. McElroy's numbers—15-for-34, 147 yards passing—were modest, but he limited the killer mistakes that did in Snead.

Snead ended the day 11-for-34 for 140 yards and four interceptions, one each by Arenas, Justin Woodall, Kareem Jackson, and Rolando McClain. Alabama also held McCluster, Ole Miss' all-purpose standout, to only 37 yards combined rushing and receiving.

"This was the most complete win we've had all year, in a difficult situation," Saban said. "It's like climbing a mountain. The higher you go the more treacherous it gets."

The Crimson Tide still had a ways to go to prove that it was still King of the Mountain in the SEC West. But on this day in Oxford, Alabama proved without a doubt that Ole Miss was not yet ready to contend for the throne. ●

No. 3 Alabama at No. 20 Mississippi

	1	2	3	4	Final
Alabama	3	13	3	3	22
Record: 6–0, 3–0 SEC					
Mississippi	0	0	3	0	3
Record: 3–2, 1–2 SEC					

When they needed him, Ingram carried the Alabama offense on his back. After Ole Miss failed to get a first down in the first half but somehow remained only nine points down, Ingram made a 36-yard touchdown run to knock out the Rebels.

Ingram Right on the Mark

Heading into the 2009 season, Mark Ingram wasn't the first name one would consider when going over potential Heisman Trophy candidates on the Crimson Tide roster. He probably wasn't second or third, either. Wide receiver Julio Jones, a record-setter as a freshman last season, was perhaps most-likely to be in the running for postseason honors. Greg McElroy was entering his first season as a starter, but quarterbacks on national-championship contenders always get Heisman attention if they have big seasons.

Alabama also had a couple of defensive players, defensive tackle Terrence Cody and linebacker Rolando McClain, who might finish in the Top 10 for the Heisman if they put together outstanding seasons. Considering that neither Alabama nor Crimson Tide head coach Nick Saban had ever had a Heisman Trophy winner, a Top 10 finish wouldn't be anything to disregard.

But as the 2009 regular season wound down, Ingram's name began to climb up the list of Heisman Trophy front-runners. In keeping with his low-key personality, the Alabama running back took all the extra attention in stride. "People bring it up all the time, and hear it all throughout my day," Ingram said. "I let everyone else do the talking on that, and stay focused on the task at hand."

Ingram didn't have to talk himself up. His teammates and opponents were more than willing to do that.

Witness LSU running back Kelvin Sheppard, whose team allowed 144 yards rushing to Ingram on November 7. But Sheppard was just as impressed with Ingram before he faced the Tigers, raving to the (New Orleans) Times-Picayune about the 5-foot-10, 212-pound sophomore from Flint, Michigan.

"Mark is the best I've seen in the conference," Sheppard said. "He's a guy who can easily go for 250 yards on any given Saturday. He runs downhill, breaks tackles, and still has speed to get on the edge. Mark does it all. I've seen him make guys miss, break tackles, spin out of the hole, run the Wildcat. He's a complete football player."

Ingram's season began with a 150-yard outing against Virginia Tech, in which he scored a touchdown both rushing and receiving in Alabama's 34–24 victory. After three less (statistically) overwhelming outings in blowout Crimson Tide wins, he reeled off six 100-yard performances in his next seven games. (The lone game less than

When he's done running over, around, and through them, Mark Ingram usually draws praise from opposing players. His versatility enables him to be successful nearly every Saturday, as he modifies his running style for each team he faces.

Though there were bigger names on the Crimson Tide roster coming into the year, no player stood out more in 2009 than Mark Ingram. He forced opposing teams to focus their game plan on him throughout his Heisman-caliber season.

00 yards was a 99-yard effort against Tennessee.)

Ingram's national coming out party came on October 17 against South Carolina, when he completely took over a 20–6 Alabama win. He rushed for 246 yards and a touchdown on 24 carries, the third-best yardage total in Crimson Tide history and a Bryant-Denny Stadium record. Ingram put the game away on a six-play touchdown drive near the end of the game, when he ran the ball on every snap. The first five of those plays came out of the Wildcat formation, a new wrinkle in the Alabama offense this season that featured Ingram taking a direct snap in the shotgun.

"If I was coach Saban, I think I would have done it [gone to the Wildcat] in the second quarter," South Carolina coach Steve Spurrier said. "They were running the ball well. If we can get a back that can go 246 some night we're going to be in good shape at South Carolina against a good defense."

Ingram is also a finalist for the Doak Walker and Maxwell Awards, the former of which goes to the top running back in the country. The Maxwell is given to the top player in all of college football, and Ingram joined Florida's Tim Tebow and Texas' Colt McCoy—a pair of quarterbacks—as the top three candidates for that award.

Ingram should erase Bobby Humphrey's school record for single-season rushing yards by season's end, not bad for a player who had never started a college game before this year. He spent the 2008 season as an understudy to Glen Coffee, but still rushed for 728 yards and an Alabama freshman record 12 touchdowns. Coffee moved on to the NFL's San Francisco 49ers this season, and Ingram moved seamlessly into the starting lineup.

"You just can't say enough about the kid," Alabama guard Mike Johnson said. "He came in last year and busted on the scene. The way he's kind of taking the reins of the ground game this year, just playing with his blockers and cutting back, the vision he displays on a day-to-day basis is just huge. He can break records and do a lot of great things around here."

Ingram was a member of Alabama's decorated 2008 signing class, but was not nearly as renowned when he joined the Crimson Tide team as were players such as Jones, quarterback Star Jackson, and linebacker Jerrell Harris, among others. If the common fan knew anything about Ingram, it was that his father, Mark Sr. played for Saban at Michigan State and spent many years in the NFL.

As he did with Coffee in 2008, Ingram is also sharing the load with a freshman this season. First-year standout Trent Richardson has shown flashes of big-play ability as Alabama's No. 2 running back, and Ingram has been among the first to great him each time he does.

"Mark's great in all aspects," McElroy said. "He's a really good person and a really hard worker. He's a really good teammate and a really good guy to have in the backfield. One thing that I will say about Mark is that he takes as much pride in his blocking and protection assignments as he does in running the ball. He is as happy when you score a touchdown via the pass as he is when he runs it in himself, so he's real quick to credit success to other people around him. He's got a great mentality in what we're trying to accomplish around here, and that's a team mindset—as long as we score points it doesn't matter who does it."

But more often than not in 2009, it's been Ingram carrying that load. ●

Ingram started the party early against Kentucky, scoring a touchdown in the first minute of the game en route to 140 total rushing yards. It was against South Carolina, however, that he truly ran into the national spotlight.

Ingram Runs Wild on Homecoming

Alabama 20, South Carolina 6 • October 17, 2009 • Tuscaloosa, Alabama

With a perfect 6–0 record through the first half of the regular season, Alabama's national championship run was beginning to pick up steam. Alabama had moved up to No. 2 in the Associated Press media rankings headed into the October 17 South Carolina game, though it held steady at No. 3 in the *USA Today* coaches' rankings. Though only the coaches poll counted in the all-important Bowl Championship Series rankings—due out the day after the South Carolina game—the fact that the Crimson Tide had slipped into the top two of the writers' poll was a good barometer of the national perception of Alabama and its place in the national championship race.

The team's perfect record also meant individual accolades were starting to pour in for Crimson Tide players. Linebacker Rolando McClain was named a semifinalist for both the Butkus (top linebacker) and Lombardi (top linebacker/lineman) Awards during South Carolina week, while defensive tackle Terrence Cody also earned a spot among the 12 Lombardi semifinalists.

The Alabama–South Carolina game was not only the Crimson Tide's homecoming but pitted against each other two of the top coaches in recent Southeastern Conference history. Alabama coach Nick Saban and South Carolina coach Steve Spurrier both won national championships at previous stops (Saban at LSU in 2003 and Spurrier at Florida in 1996), and had a combined eight SEC championships on their resumes.

"I've known Steve for a long time," said Saban, who carried a 0–2 career record against Spurrier into this year's meeting. "I was his assistant in the East-West (college all-star) game years ago.… I have a lot of respect for him. He has done a great job every place he has been. We played against him at LSU when he was still at Florida. I think he is an outstanding coach and has done a really job at South Carolina."

South Carolina sported a 5–1 record coming in, with the only loss in shootout fashion to Georgia. Like Alabama, the Gamecocks had defensively dominated preseason SEC West favorite Ole Miss, winning 16–10 to catapult themselves in the national Top 25.

But it wasn't defense that ruled this day. Instead it was a budding offensive superstar for Alabama, whose one-man show sent him skyrocketing into the forefront

The star of the show was Mark Ingram. He torched the Gamecock defense for 246 yards–third best total in school history–and took direct snaps five plays in a row on the game's decisive drive.

of the Heisman Trophy race after the Crimson Tide's 20–6 win over the Gamecocks.

Alabama sophomore Mark Ingram, who had been a picture of steady excellence through the season's first six games, broke through with an otherworldly performance against the Gamecocks. He set a new career-high with 246 yards and a touchdown on 24 carries, with the yardage total the third-highest in Crimson Tide history and the best-ever at Bryant-Denny Stadium. Only Shaun Alexander (291 yards at LSU in 1999) and Bobby Humphrey (284 at Mississippi State in 1986) had posted higher single-game yardage totals than Ingram did against South Carolina.

"Mark Ingram was fantastic," Saban said. "The guy ran with tremendous passion and heart and did a wonderful job out there. If we had (a roster full of) guys that could play like that, the sky would be the limit."

Not that Alabama's defense didn't do its part as well. Despite the absence of star cornerback Javier Arenas, who was sidelined with bruised ribs, the Crimson Tide held its opponent out of the end zone for the second straight week.

Alabama's defense was also responsible for the game's first score, which came on the second play after the opening kickoff. Safety Mark Barron intercepted a Stephen Garcia throw deep down the middle and returned it 77 yards for a touchdown, giving the Crimson Tide a 7–0 lead just 1:02 into the game.

Alabama turned the ball over itself on its first two possessions, with quarterback Greg McElroy throwing a pair of uncharacteristic interceptions. But a heads-up play by wide receiver Julio Jones forced a fumble on the second one, and the Crimson Tide was able to drive for a 25-yard Leigh Tiffin field goal and a 10–0 lead after one quarter.

(above) McElroy struggled against one of the nation's best pass defenses, throwing a pair of interceptions. (opposite) While Mark Ingram made the headlines, other backs like Roy Upchurch got into the party as well in Alabama's 264-yard rushing day. Upchurch also caught a pair of passes for 18 yards.

South Carolina got on the board with a 22-yard Spencer Lanning field goal in the second quarter to cut it to 10-3, with Alabama's Marquis Johnson keeping the Gamecocks out of the end zone by knocking away three consecutive passes intended for Alshon Jeffery. Ingram then carried the Crimson Tide to a score late in the half, breaking free for a 54-yard run deep into Gamecocks territory, which set up Tiffin's 35-yard field goal and a 13–3 lead.

The Gamecocks got Lanning's 31-yard field goal on the final play of the half to make it 13–6, but that would be all the scoring for a while. Each team made big defensive stands in the third quarter—South Carolina forcing a McElroy fumble and Alabama sacking Garcia to knock the Gamecocks out of field goal range—to keep it a 7-point game headed into the fourth quarter.

Finally, midway through the fourth quarter, Alabama put the game away with a touchdown drive. This one was all Ingram, as he kept the ball five straight times out of the Wildcat formation—including runs of 22 and 24 yards—before taking a pitch from McElroy and racing into the end zone from four yards out for the touchdown with 4:54 to play.

Just for good measure, the Crimson Tide made a late defensive stand to keep South Carolina from scoring a touchdown, as Johnson and Kareem Jackson broke up passes in the end zone in the game's final moments. Alabama had its two-touchdown win and a 7–0 record, with the all-important arch-rivalry showdown with Tennessee up next. ●

No. 2 Alabama vs. No. 22 South Carolina

	1	2	3	4	Final
South Carolina	0	6	0	0	6
Record: 5–2, 2–2 SEC					
Alabama	10	3	0	7	20
Record: 7–0, 4–0 SEC					

Mark Ingram bowled over anyone and everyone, with this touchdown serving as an exclamation point, in the win over South Carolina.

Cody Saves the Day

Alabama 12, Tennessee 10 • October 24, 2009 • Tuscaloosa, Alabama

Nearly every championship team has at least one—a game that might very well have been a loss had one play or another gone the other way. Alabama's 1992 national-championship squad trailed in the fourth quarter against Mississippi State before coming back and winning and needed a late David Palmer punt return to put away lowly Louisiana Tech. The Crimson Tide's 1979 national-title squad won 3–0 at LSU and trailed Tennessee 17–0 early before rallying for victory.

Likewise, the 2009 Alabama football team had its "uh-oh" moment, and it came with the clock ticking down against Tennessee on October 24. The unranked Volunteers lined up for a 44-yard field goal attempt, which would give them a one-point win if it was good.

But Daniel Lincoln's kick crashed right into the side of a mountain, as Alabama nose tackle Terrence "Mount" Cody thrust his gigantic left arm between the football and the goal posts to preserve a 12–10 Crimson Tide victory. Cody's block was his second of the fourth quarter, and preserved Alabama's perfect 8–0 record and kept it in the driver's seat for its SEC and national championship runs.

"I didn't really get off the ground," Cody said. "I just reached my arm up. That's how I got it. I knocked (the blocker) back. He was on his back."

The play known as "Maximum Block" was a near-perfect special-teams execution by the Crimson Tide, which also got backfield penetration by corner rushers Kareem Jackson and Javier Arenas. Julio Jones also got high in the air behind Cody, and might have blocked the kick if Cody didn't.

Nevertheless, the fact that Cody was even in a position to save the game was the result of a terrible few minutes of football by Alabama, beginning with an uncharacteristic mistake by one of the team's best players. The Crimson Tide led 12–3 with less than four minutes to play, and seemed to have sealed the game after Tennessee was called for roughing the punter to extend an Alabama possession. But Alabama's Mark Ingram fumbled on the next play, the first lost fumble of his career. Tennessee had new life and the football at the Crimson Tide's 43-yard line with 3:29 left in the game.

Tennessee converted a pair of third downs on the drive, including Jonathan Crompton's 11-yard touch-

Ingram chugged for 99 yards on 18 carries in yet another impressive performance. Along with the rest of the offense, however, he was unable to find the end zone against a stout Tennessee defense.

down pass to Gerald Jones, which cut the Tide advantage to two. The Volunteers then recovered an onside kick, as the ball bounced off the hands of Alabama's Julio Jones and into the arms of a Tennessee player.

The Volunteers got two first downs, including a 27-yard pass from Crompton to tight end Luke Stocker to move the ball inside the Alabama 30. Tennessee, which had no timeouts remaining, worked into field-goal position, setting the stage for Cody's now-legendary game-saving play.

"You talk about how fragile a season is," Alabama coach Nick Saban said. "You're controlling a game, even though you may say it's winning ugly. We're still ahead 12–3 and totally controlling the game with 3 minutes, 29 seconds and the ball. That's how fragile a season can be. You make one mistake and you have to go overcome it. I hope that there's a lot of lessons our team can learn from this."

As Saban said, the entire game was ugly for Alabama, at least on offense. The Crimson Tide gained a season-low 256 yards of total offense and failed to score a touchdown for the first time all year.

Leigh Tiffin bailed out the Alabama offense with four field goals, continuing a personal hot streak, having missed just one field goal dating back to the North Texas game. Ingram rushed for 99 yards on 18 carries before the fumble, and quarterback Greg McElroy threw for just 120 yards.

Tennessee managed 339 yards of total offense, but did not score a touchdown until 1:19 left in the game. The Alabama defense limited the Vols to 74 yards rushing, and forced four Lincoln field-goal attempts, of which he made only one.

Cody also blocked a 43-yard field-goal attempt early in the fourth quarter, and Lincoln came up short on

Jonathan Crompton was harassed all day by the Alabama defense but had an efficient day passing—including throwing for the game's only touchdown.

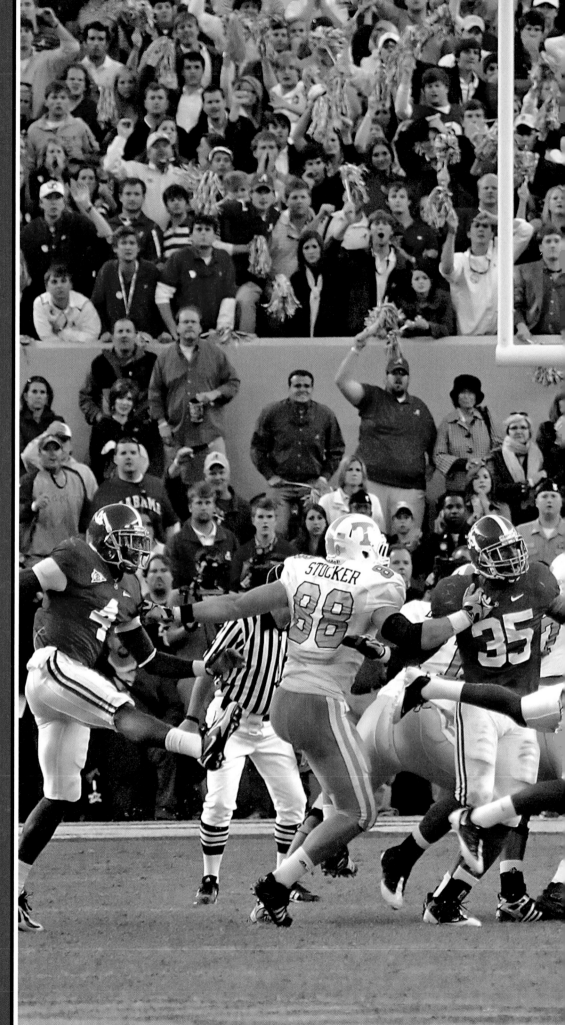

It helps to have a mountain in the middle: Terrence Cody blocked two Tennessee field goal attempts in the fourth quarter. There may have been no bigger single play in the championship season than the second block, sealing the win for the Tide.

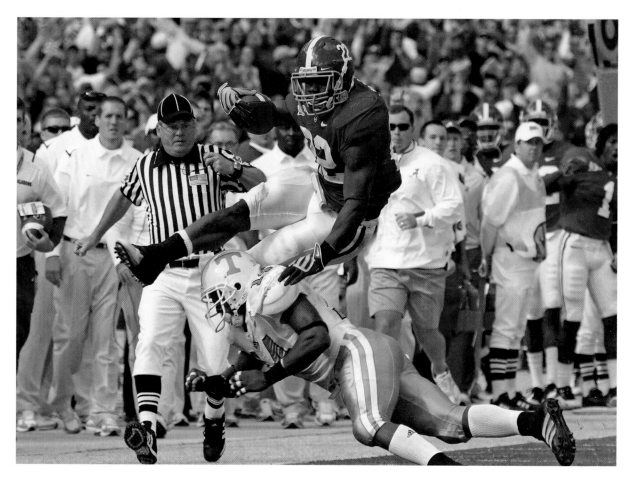

a 49-yarder at the end of the first half. That was in sharp contrast to Tiffin, who was perfect on kicks of 38, 50, 22, and 49.

"He did a fantastic job," Saban said. "He made four field goals today, two of them 50-yarders, and there was a little bit of wind out there—it's pretty much a crosswind in our stadium—he negotiated both of those and did a great job of hitting them. It was the difference in the game guys, those two fields goals and the ones we blocked."

Cody's second blocked kick brought to mind a memorable 11–10 win over Tennessee in 1966, when the Vols missed a potential winning kick in the game's final moments. That victory in Knoxville also kept the Crimson Tide undefeated, and Alabama would end the year 11–0.

This year's win over Tennessee took Alabama—ranked No. 2 in the first edition of the Bowl Championship Series rankings—into a much-needed bye week, with a Top 10 showdown against LSU coming up two weeks later.

"Every game we are just trying to get better," Ingram said. "We are showing up at times but we also have things to work on. I think we are starting to mold together as a group." ●

No. 2 Alabama vs. Tennessee

	1	2	3	4	Final
Tennessee	0	3	0	7	10
Record: 3–4, 1–3					
Alabama	3	6	0	3	12
Record: 8–0, 5–0					

(above) Tennessee's defense stood up respectably to the Crimson Tide and even forced Ingram's first collegiate fumble. (opposite) Nearly half of McElroy's passing yards went to Julio Jones, who had seven catches.

Kings of the West Again

Alabama 24, LSU 15 • November 7, 2009 • Tuscaloosa, Alabama

The celebration resulting from the 12–10 victory over Tennessee had an extra few days to die down, as Alabama had its only bye week of the season the following Saturday. But after some recovery time, it was back to work against another archrival, with No. 9 LSU coming to town for a nationally televised match-up on November 7.

Alabama's players picked up plenty of individual accolades during the down period. Colin Peek was named a semifinalist for both the Mackey (top tight end) and Wuerffel (community service) Awards, while fellow senior Javier Arenas was named a semifinalist for the Thorpe Award (top defensive back). Four Alabama players were also named Mid-Season All-Americans by *The Sporting News:* Arenas, running back Mark Ingram, offensive guard Mike Johnson, and defensive tackle Terrence Cody. Ingram, who was approaching the 1,000-yard mark, was also gaining steam in the Heisman Trophy race.

The off-field news was not all positive, however, as Alabama dropped to No. 3 in the Bowl Championship Rankings behind Florida and Texas during its bye week. Nevertheless, the Crimson Tide would still have a shot at the Gators by winning the Southeastern Conference West Division championship, which it could wrap up by beating LSU.

As always, LSU was a quality SEC West contender, having lost only to Florida, 13–3 on October 10. The Tigers had won four straight times in Tuscaloosa, dating back to a 23–16 Alabama win in 1999.

That was the year before Nick Saban took over as head coach at LSU, where he went 48–16 and won the 2003 national championship during a five-year tenure in Baton Rouge. His presence now on the Alabama sideline always adds a level of intrigue when the Crimson Tide and Tigers play, but Saban was quick to dismiss any such distractions.

"The game is about the players," Saban said. "There are a lot of good players. These are two very good teams that have good players on both sides and there is a lot to talk about in terms of what's going to happen on the field. Our focus needs to be on us playing our best football of the year, and that's certainly what we're going to try and coach to get our players to do."

Alabama emerged with a 24–15 victory to earn its

No, it's not Tom Hanks starring as Forrest Gump, it's Darius Hanks hauling in McElroy's pass from 21 yards out for a third-quarter touchdown that put Alabama ahead 10–7.

seventh SEC West championship and a December date with Florida, but it wasn't easy. The Crimson Tide scored the game's final 14 points and overcame some tense moments in the fourth to garner its second straight win over Saban's old team. Alabama outgained LSU 452 yards to 253 and left the Tigers battered and bruised. The Crimson Tide's stalwart defense knocked LSU starting quarterback Jordan Jefferson (ankle) and running back Charles Scott (shoulder) from the game with injuries.

The two teams traded punts for the entire first quarter, before LSU finally put together a touchdown drive early in the second. The Tigers drove 91 yards in 13 plays, with Jefferson hitting DeAngelo Peterson for a 12-yard touchdown to put LSU up 7–0.

Alabama managed only Leigh Tiffin's 28-yard field goal to make it 7–3 at the half. Tiffin had now scored 22 of the Crimson Tide's last 28 points dating back to the first quarter of the South Carolina game, but the Alabama offense finally got cranked up in the third quarter against LSU.

Ingram rushed three times for 42 yards on Alabama's 63-yard scoring drive following the second-half kickoff, and Greg McElroy hit Darius Hanks on a 21-yard touchdown pass. Following Tiffin's extra point, the Crimson Tide led 10–7 with 11:40 left in the third.

LSU punter Josh Jasper soon pinned Alabama at its own 1-yard line, allowing the Tigers' defense to temporarily turn the game. McElroy was called for intentional grounding in the end zone, resulting in a safety to pull LSU within 10–9 with 5:55 to go in the third quarter.

The Tigers took the free kick and came right back with a touchdown, moving into position on Scott's 34-yard run. Scott was knocked out of the game with what would prove to be a broken collarbone on the play, but two plays later, back-up tailback Stevan Ridley raced into the end zone from eight yards away to give LSU a 15–10 advantage. The Tigers went for two but did not make it, as safety Mark Barron knocked down Jarrett Lee's pass in the end zone.

Alabama got back within 15–13 on Tiffin's 20-yard

(above) McElroy was well-protected against LSU, a must when passing against a team with such a strong secondary. He was intercepted once but was solid all game, completing 19 passes for 276 yards and a pair of touchdowns. (opposite) Mark Ingram posted a 6.5-yards-per-carry average against LSU—144 yards on 22 carries. He also caught five passes out of the backfield for 50 yards.

Julio Jones races downfield for the deciding touchdown in the fourth quarter against LSU. Jones broke free after the catch on a short-yardage route, and Tigers defenders could only nip at his heels as he sped to the end zone.

field goal with 12:35 remaining, and the Tide needed just one play to take the lead after forcing LSU to go 3-and-out and punt. McElroy faked to his left and fired quickly back to his right to Jones, who shook a tackle near the line of scrimmage and sprinted 73 yards for a touchdown. Trent Richardson bolted into the end zone for two points, and Alabama led 21–15 with 10:24 to play.

Alabama quickly forced another punt, then came the controversy. After a running-into-the-punter penalty kept the Crimson Tide drive alive (Alabama converted a fourth-and-1 on the next play rather than punting), LSU defensive back Patrick Peterson appeared to intercept a pass near the sideline. The play was ruled out of bounds on the field, and replay review upheld the call, much to the Tigers' chagrin.

Alabama drove down and got in position for Tiffin's 40-yard field goal, which gave the Tide a 9-point lead with 3:04 to play. Robby Green's interception with 2:04 remaining slammed the door on any potential LSU comeback.

Ingram ended the night with 144 yards rushing on 25 carries, while Jones caught four passes for 102 yards. McElroy threw for 276 yards and two touchdowns, his best performance in weeks.

"We've been practicing hard all week for this game," wide receiver Marquis Maze said. "We saw that we could beat them in the passing game, but they (LSU) played a heck of a game. We just came out and executed and did what we were supposed to do. We all made the plays we were supposed to make." ●

No. 3 Alabama vs. LSU

	1	2	3	4	Final
LSU	0	7	8	0	15
Record: 7–2, 4–2					
Alabama	0	3	7	14	24
Record: 9–0, 6–0					

In the fourth quarter, the Crimson Tide rode the legs of Mark Ingram into scoring range. A Leigh Tiffin field goal iced the win, Alabama's fist home victory against LSU since 1999.

The Big Crimson Wall

Dan Mullen's Mississippi State team was fairly typical among Alabama's opponents this season. Mullen's Bulldogs gained just 213 yards of total offense and turned the ball over three times. Mississippi State lost 31–3, one of six Alabama opponents held to single digits among the season's first 11 games.

When Mullen watched his Bulldogs try to move the ball against Alabama, he didn't see 11 players in crimson helmets moving around the field. He saw a big crimson wall. "They are big, and they are physical," Mullen said. "They have a lot of size and what they do is just try to create a wall right there, and there's not a whole lot of seams in the wall for you to run through."

It's a common pastime among Alabama fans to compare any good defense to the legendary one the Crimson Tide fielded in its national-championship season of 1992. Alabama led the country in all four major defensive categories (total defense, rushing defense, passing defense, and scoring defense) at the end of the regular season that year, and that unit eventually sent eight of its 11 starters on to the NFL.

The Crimson Tide has fielded some fine defenses in the years since—including in 1994, 1996, 1999, 2002, 2005, and 2008. But this year's defense perhaps comes closer than most to that one from 17 seasons ago, and does so because it possesses one quality in overwhelming amounts: speed. "This is the fastest defense if you went from (players) 1 to 11," Ole Miss coach Houston Nutt said. "From corners to safeties to linebackers to defensive linemen, this is the best I've seen."

Alabama's defensive success starts up front, with three stout men along the line in the Nick Saban's 3–4 scheme. Ends Lorenzo Washington, Brandon Deaderick, and Marcell Dareus are all between 6-foot-3 and 6-foot-5, and between 280 and 290 pounds, big enough to hold the point against the run, but not so big as to keep them from being factors as pass-rushers.

But the key man on the line is right in the middle, a 6-foot-5, 360-pound mass of humanity named Terrence Cody. The junior-college transfer was a first-team All-American in 2008, and is a finalist for both the Bednarik and Lombardi Awards given to the top defensive player and top lineman, respectively, in college football.

Cody plugs up the middle like no player in college football, tying up more than one blocker on most plays and freeing up the Alabama linebackers to make tack-

Opposing teams would have been better served to forget about running between the tackles in 2009. Consensus All-American Cody consumes so much space that the rest of the defense can swarm to the ball virtually unimpeded.

Terrence Cody is the big man—figuratively as well as literally—on the Alabama defensive line but the whole unit is stout. Marcell Dareus was an impact player as a sophomore, leading the team in sacks during the regular season with 6.5.

es. He'll almost certainly be a first-round pick in April's NFL draft. "He's just a big guy and so athletic," Virginia Tech coach Frank Beamer said. "I'd say he's real difficult (to block). I think a lot of people have tried without much success. I think he's a heck of a football player."

Linebacker is another position loaded with role players, from converted safety Cory Reamer at Sam (strong side) to pass-rushing specialist Eryk Anders at Jack (a combination of linebacker and defensive end). Potential All-American Dont'a Hightower—the Crimson Tide's starting Will (weak side) linebacker—went down with a knee injury in Week 4 against Arkansas, but freshman Nico Johnson has filled in ably and shown some flashes of star ability in his own right.

That leaves Mike (middle) linebacker, and the person who has manned that position for the last three seasons for Alabama is Rolando McClain. The 6-foot-4, 258-pound junior took over as a starter early in his freshman season, and has been a dominant force ever since. McClain was a first-team All-Southeastern Conference pick in 2008, and is well on his way to even further accolades this season. He'll almost certainly be a first-team All-American, with a chance to win the Butkus Award (best linebacker in the country) and SEC Defensive Player of the Year honors.

As Cody did a year ago, McClain will have a major decision following the season as to whether or not to enter the NFL draft. He possesses the ability to take over a game like few other players in the country. "From tackle-to-tackle, I haven't seen one better," Nutt said of McClain. "And then he has skills to go catch the ball, intercept the ball, knock balls down. He is a big-time force. I can tell he's a big-time leader and

one of the best in the SEC if not the best."

The secondary is Saban's personal stomping ground and it's common to see the head coach working one-on-one with Crimson Tide defensive backs during each Alabama practice. His 2009 team features another outstanding secondary, a group equally skilled in both run support and pass defense.

Cornerback Kareem Jackson and free safety Justin Woodall are multiyear starters, while nickel cornerback Marquis Johnson has been a contributor for three seasons. Sophomore strong safety Mark Barron has shown flashes of star potential in his first season as a regular, leading the team in interceptions and developing a reputation as a big hitter.

But the key man might just be someone who was once viewed as nothing more than a return specialist, a 5-foot-9, 198-pound ball of electricity and swagger, cornerback Javier Arenas. The senior might be the SEC's all-time leader in punt returns for touchdowns, but is also nearly as accomplished as a defensive player.

Arenas became a starter as a junior in 2008, and brought many of the same skills that helped him excel in the return game to the defensive side of the ball. His brute strength makes him one of the Crimson Tide's surest tacklers, while his quickness helps him stay in the face of opposing receivers and quarterbacks.

"Javy's a great competitor," defensive coordinator Kirby Smart said. "It bothers him when someone completes a five-yard out against him. He gets motivated through a fear of failure and competitive nature. He's probably the strongest guy on the team pound-for-pound and that gives him the ability to compete every day."

From front to back and side to side, there's just no hole in the Big Crimson Wall. •

The defense was a force to be reckoned with from all angles. Here, Mark Barron returns an interception, with an escort of teammates, for a touchdown against South Carolina.

10-0 Once Again

Alabama 31, Mississippi State 3 • November 14, 2009 • Starkville, Mississippi

As Alabama headed into the final three-game stretch of its regular season, the Crimson Tide was in firm grasp of its championship destiny. Alabama had already clinched the Southeastern Conference West Division, meaning an SEC championship game showdown with top-ranked Florida was in the offing. And having moved up to No. 2 in the most-recent Bowl Championship Series rankings, the Crimson Tide's mission was clear: win its last four games including the SEC championship, and play for the national title.

That path to glory continued with a road trip to Starkville, Mississippi, to face Mississippi State, historically a team that Alabama had dominated. The Bulldogs did win three straight over the Tide in the late-1990s and two in a row in 2006 and 2007, but otherwise, MSU victories over Alabama were rare.

This year's Mississippi State team came in at 4–5 under new coach Dan Mullen, who had previously served as Florida's offensive coordinator. Many in the Alabama camp believed facing the Bulldogs would serve as good practice for the Gators, who run similar offensive and defensive systems, albeit with more talent.

"Dan Mullen has done a really good job with this team," Alabama coach Nick Saban said. "Of their five losses, every team has been a top 25 team that they have lost to and four of them are currently ranked in the top 10 or 12, or something like that.… They have sort of a Florida spread philosophy and it's a little difficult, different preparation, so our players are going to have to have to do a really good job of getting prepared for this game and getting ready to stop the plays that they run, because they are not always conventional-type things that you see all the time. Their defense plays hard, very physical and tough. It will be a challenge for us."

The individual accolades continued to roll in for Alabama during game week, with defensive lineman Terrence Cody named a finalist for the Lombardi Award (best defensive lineman/linebacker). Also named semifinalists for national awards were Leigh Tiffin for the Lou Groza Award (top kicker), Mark Ingram for the Doak Walker Award (top running back), and Rolando McClain for the Lott Trophy (defensive player who displays excellence in athletics, academics, and community service).

Playing before a record-crowd of 58,103 at Mississippi

There was no need to let up on the gas even if the SEC West was already won—Darius Hanks took this pass down the sideline for a 45-yard score early in the second quarter, and the points proved to be decisive.

State's Scott Field, Alabama put forth one of its more-dominant performances of the year in a 31–3 victory. The Crimson Tide outgained the Bulldogs 444 yards to 212 and held its opponent without a touchdown for the third time in five games.

The victory lifted Alabama to 10–0 for the second straight season, the first time the Crimson Tide had done so since 1973–74. It was also the first time Alabama had achieved back-to-back 10-win seasons since 1991–92, and it was the first time Saban had done so in his coaching career.

"We're jelling as a team, not overlooking the small things," wide receiver Marquis Maze said. "We fought hard all night and executed really well, I thought. That's what it's all about."

Ingram continued to make his Heisman Trophy case with 149 yards and two touchdowns on 19 carries, his sixth 100-yard outing of the season and fifth in six weeks. He left the game briefly in the second quarter after opening a gash that required eight stitches over his right eye, an injury that occurred when his helmet was knocked off during a 1-yard touchdown run.

Aside from Ingram's short TD run, Alabama's other three touchdowns came from 45 yards or longer. Two of those scores came on one-play drives in the fourth quarter, a 48-yard pass from Greg McElroy to Julio Jones and a 70-yard run by Ingram. "Three yards and a cloud of dust is pretty much the staple of our offense," McElroy said. "But we have the ability to break it for a big play."

After going scoreless in the first quarter for the second straight game, Alabama broke through with two touchdowns in the second period to grab a 14–0 halftime lead. The Crimson Tide moved 80 yards in six plays for the first, with McElroy connecting with Hanks in the left flat, and Hanks shaking loose for a 48-yard touchdown to

The Crimson Tide defense was stubborn as usual, holding the Bulldogs to just 213 yards of offense. Mark Barron led the defense by picking off a pair of passes while Marquis Johnson also had a strong game, including an interception.

put Alabama up 7–0 with 12:48 left in the first half.

Alabama then forced a Mississippi State punt and drove 11 plays and 72 yards for its second touchdown. The biggest play was an 11-yard strike from McElroy to Hanks on third-and-7, and Ingram punched the ball in from the 1 to make it 14–0.

The Crimson Tide went up 17–0 on Leigh Tiffin's 39-yard field goal in the third quarter, a score set up by a 42-yard pass from McElroy to Maze. McElroy ended the night 13-for-18 passing, for 192 yards and two touchdowns.

Mississippi State then drove into Alabama territory three straight times, but could come up with only Derek DePasquale's 34-yard field goal to make it 17–3 with 10:35 remaining. The Crimson Tide went right to the air to put the game away after Javier Arenas returned the kickoff 46 yards, with McElroy hitting a wide-open Jones for a 48-yard score and a 24–3 lead.

Mark Barron intercepted Tyson Lee on MSU's next possession, Barron's second interception of the game and one of three by the Crimson Tide on the night. Ingram shot through the middle of the Bulldogs' defense for a 70-yard score on the next play, and Alabama had its 28-point margin of victory with 7:24 to play.

It was a complete victory for the Crimson Tide, and moved the team one step closer to a potential national championship. ●

No. 2 Alabama at Mississippi State

	1	2	3	4	Final
Alabama	0	14	3	14	31
Record: 10–0, 7–0					
Miss. State	0	0	0	3	3
Record: 4–6, 2–4					

(above) It was no surprise that Leigh Tiffin made a run at the Groza Award as a senior. The fine placekicker didn't have much work against Mississippi State but did add another field goal, one of 25 he kicked during the regular season. (opposite) Even when they threatened, the Bulldogs were thwarted by timely Alabama defensive plays. In addition to his interception, Marquis Johnson batted down a pair of balls in the end zone.

A Shutout and a Big Send-Off

Alabama 45, Chattanooga 0 • November 21, 2009 • Tuscaloosa, Alabama

After seven straight weeks of facing Southeastern Conference teams, Alabama took a decided downturn in competition for its final home game of the season. Chattanooga, a member of the NCAA Football Championship Subdivision (formerly Division I-AA), came calling on November 21 at Bryant-Denny Stadium for a game in which Alabama could likely have named its score. The Crimson Tide more or less did just that, scoring touchdowns on five consecutive possessions in the first half and giving its 27 seniors a big send-off in their final home game with a 45–0 victory.

Alabama, which had stayed No. 2 behind Florida in the Bowl Championship Series rankings for the second straight week, also managed to avoid major injury in the game. The Crimson Tide used 77 players in all, pulling most of its starters by halftime.

Even though the chances of an upset were infinitesimal, Alabama coach Nick Saban knew just what buttons to push to make sure his team was properly motivated to face the Mocs. "I told the players if we had lost this game today, there would be nothing else that would tarnish what you've accomplished more than that," Saban said. "You would someday be an NFL player in a Mercedes-Benz and roll your window down to talk to a pretty girl and she'd say, 'You lost to Chattanooga when you played at Alabama.' Nobody would ever forget that one."

Instead, Alabama put Chattanooga away with a three-touchdown barrage in the final five minutes of the first quarter. Trent Richardson started the scoring with a 2-yard touchdown run, then Mark Ingram made it 14–0 with a 25-yard score of his own. After Cory Reamer intercepted Chattanooga quarterback B.J. Coleman and returned the ball to the Mocs' 31, Greg McElroy went up top for a 19-yard scoring strike to Julio Jones.

The Crimson Tide took a four-touchdown lead on the third play of the second quarter, when Javier Arenas ran a punt back 66 yards for a touchdown. The score was Arenas' first of the year and seventh of his career, breaking the Southeastern Conference record formerly held by Kentucky's Derek Abney. Arenas would earn SEC Special Teams Player of the Week honors for his performance, which also featured an interception and two pass breakups on defense.

The Mocs were clearly overmatched by the Crimson Tide from the opening kickoff. As a result, the 27 Alabama seniors, including Roy Upchurch, were able to say good-bye to Bryant-Denny Stadium in style. Upchurch recorded a touchdown and 70 yards rushing during his 17-carry finale.

"Everybody executed, which made my job much easier," Arenas said. "I didn't have that many tackles to break off on the punt return game, and I just played my assignment on defense."

Alabama added another touchdown before halftime on Mark Ingram's 40-yard run with 9:53 left in the second to make it 35–0. That would be the Heisman Trophy candidate's final action of the day, but he finished with 102 yards and two scores on 11 carries.

Alabama scored twice in the second half, on Leigh Tiffin's 41-yard field goal and Roy Upchurch's 21-yard run. Back-up quarterback Star Jackson ran the offense for all but the final series of the second half (when third-stringer Thomas Darrah came in), and completed 4 of 5 passes for 29 yards in relief of McElroy, who was 6-for-11 for 80 yards and a score.

The Crimson Tide defense, led by Butkus Award finalist Rolando McClain and Nagurski Award finalist Terrence Cody, held the Mocs to 84 yards of total offense and five first downs, while forcing three turnovers.

Alabama's date with Florida in the SEC championship game and long been set. The only order of business remaining before meeting the Gators—and between the Crimson Tide and a second-straight 12–0 regular season—was the annual Iron Bowl showdown with Auburn set for the following Friday. ●

No. 2 Alabama vs. Chattanooga

	1	2	3	4	Final
Chattanooga	0	0	0	0	0
Record: 6–5					
Alabama	21	14	3	7	45
Record: 11–0					

Julio Jones skies to haul in Greg McElroy's 19-yard touchdown pass in the first quarter. The score made it 21–0 and there was little need to pass afterwards.

The Drive

Alabama 26, Auburn 21 • November 27, 2009 • Auburn, Alabama

Add another memorable phrase to a rivalry that already included "The Kick," "Wrong Way Bo," and "Punt, Bama, Punt." Greg McElroy and the Alabama Crimson Tide have now introduced "The Drive," into Iron Bowl lore.

McElroy and the Crimson Tide drove 79 yards in 15 plays late in the fourth quarter to help Alabama beat Auburn 26–21 and finish the regular season at 12–0 for the second straight season. McElroy hit Roy Upchurch with a 4-yard touchdown pass with 1:24 remaining as the Crimson Tide overcame an early two-touchdown deficit to keep its national-championship dreams alive.

"That may have been one of the greatest drives I have ever been associated with in the fourth quarter to win the game," Alabama coach Nick Saban said. "I just can't say enough about how proud I am of our team."

The Drive began with 8:27 left in the game and Auburn leading 21–20 after the Tigers downed a punt at the Alabama 21-yard line. The Crimson Tide converted back-to-back third downs to get the ball near midfield, with McElroy hitting Julio Jones on both passes. McElroy found Jones again to get into Auburn territory,

then later hit Trent Richardson—who was subbing for an injured Mark Ingram—for 17 yards to the Tigers' 11. After two Richardson runs, the ball stood on the Auburn 4, with Alabama facing third down and 3.

That's when Saban decided to go for the touchdown, overruling his assistant coaches who wanted to run again and set up the field goal. McElroy play-faked to Richardson, then found Upchurch in the right flat for the touchdown and Alabama's first lead of the day.

"I was yelling at everybody, 'Put me in! Put me in!'" said Upchurch, an oft-injured fifth-year senior who had never caught a touchdown pass in his career. "No one was hearing me. I just had the feeling that I'd be wide open in the end zone. They changed the play. Patience pays off, and today I've got a story to tell."

Alabama failed on a two-point-conversion attempt, meaning the Tide led by only five and would have to hold on defensively for the win. Auburn drove as far as the Alabama 37, but Chris Todd's last-second pass was batted down in the end zone by Justin Woodall and Rolando McClain, and the Tide had its second straight win over Auburn.

In a rivalry that has had plenty of epic moments, none may stand bigger than the climax of "The Drive" as Roy Upchurch hauled in a four-yard pass from Greg McElroy for the game's deciding points.

"The strong do survive but the strong do get their [butts] kicked," Saban said. "That was my message to the team."

While the last eight minutes was all Alabama, the Crimson Tide had to play catch-up most of the day. Auburn used its razzle-dazzle offense to post two quick touchdowns in the first quarter.

First came a 67-yard TD run on a reverse by wide receiver Terrell Zachery, who wound up the game's leading rushing despite just one carry. The Tigers then perfectly executed an onside kick, with kicker Wes Byrum recovering the ball on the Auburn 42.

The Tigers went 58 yards in 12 plays, getting the benefit of a personal foul on Woodall to keep the drive alive. Todd hit fullback Eric Smith for a 1-yard touchdown and Auburn had stunned the college football nation by taking a 14–0 lead with 5:42 left in the first quarter.

Alabama went 3-and-out on its first two possessions, but finally put together a drive beginning late in the first quarter. Richardson's 2-yard run made it 14–7 with 13:26 to go in the half.

Alabama tied the game on McElroy's 33-yard touchdown pass to Peek midway through the second quarter, but missed a chance to take the lead when Leigh Tiffin missed a 42-yard field goal. Still, for all Auburn's early fireworks, the game was tied at the half.

Auburn used its final big play to jump on top by seven in the third quarter. Todd found a wide-open Darvin Adams for a 72-yard touchdown and the Tigers led 21–14.

Javier Arenas returned a punt 56 yards to the Auburn 33, but Alabama wound up with only Tiffin's 27-yard field goal to make it 21-17. A Mark Barron interception also led to three points, with Tiffin's 31-yarder making it a one-point game after three quarters.

Upchurch had caught another pass from McElroy earlier in the game, part of an efficient passing attack that went for 218 yards on a day that the Auburn defense was able to severely limit the Crimson Tide ground game.

While Auburn's defense held fast at times, they had no answer for Jones. After a quiet season he broke out in this game, hauling in a career-high nine passes.

That score stood up until Alabama's game-winning drive. The Crimson Tide defense stood tall late in the game, holding Auburn to only 39 net yards and three first downs after Adams' touchdown.

McElroy came through with one of his finer performances of the year, hitting on 21 of 31 passes for 218 yards and two touchdowns. Jones had nine catches for 83 yards.

Ingram was held in check with only 34 yards on 16 carries before the injury, but Richardson came through in his absence. The freshman rushed for 51 yards and a touchdown on 15 carries and also caught three passes for 31 yards.

McClain led the way defensively with 12 tackles and a sack, while Eryk Anders had seven tackles, a forced fumble, a sack, and three quarterback hurries. Arenas had three tackles and a sack and totaled 113 yards in returns, becoming the SEC's all-time leader in career punt-return yards during the game.

"This team is all about character, discipline, and overcoming adversity and perseverance by our players," Saban said. "If there is one thing our team has not been challenged by this year, it's that. We didn't play a great game today. It's a great win for our team and I have never been prouder of a team in terms of the way they won." ●

No. 2 Alabama at Auburn

	1	2	3	4	Final
Alabama	0	14	6	6	26
Record: 12–0, 8–0 SEC					
Auburn	14	0	7	0	21
Record: 7–5, 3–5 SEC					

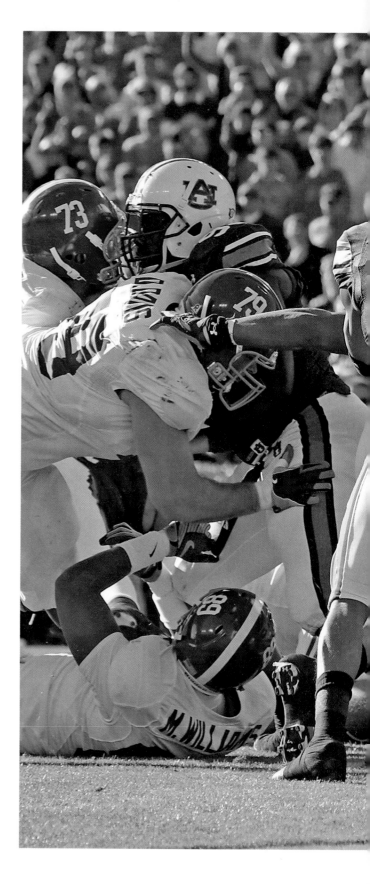

Mark Ingram was unable to get going against Auburn so it was Trent Richardson that shouldered the bulk of the load, carrying 15 times for 51 yards and this second quarter score that brought Alabama within a touchdown.

Alabama's Unsung Heroes

Mark Ingram, Greg McElroy, Julio Jones, Mike Johnson, Terrence Cody, Rolando McClain, Javier Arenas—those are the household names that have carried Alabama to the verge of its 13th national championship. But just as important to the Crimson Tide's success are names such as Drew Davis, Collin Peek, Roy Upchurch, Lorenzo Washington, Eryk Anders, Cory Reamer, Marquis Johnson, Leigh Tiffin, and Brian Selman. It is these unsung heroes who have done the team's dirty work, plugging the trenches and excelling on special teams to give Alabama's stars a chance to shine.

Of those unsung heroes, all but Peek (who transferred from Georgia Tech) are holdovers from the Mike Shula era, when Alabama struggled both to gain bowl eligibility each season and to keep itself relevant in the national college football discussion. Many were written off more than once for one reason or another, but they're all still here, playing key roles on an undefeated team that is one win away from the national championship.

When coach Nick Saban arrived prior to the 2007 season, he began stockpiling talent on the Alabama roster, thanks to three straight Top 10 recruiting classes. That made competition fierce for those who stuck around, as Reamer told The Birmingham News earlier this season.

"A lot of the guys who got recruited by the old staff really have been under question ever since the new staff got here," Reamer said. "A lot of the fans especially didn't have much faith in us. They all thought we weren't going to do very well as a team, that we would be good once coach Saban got his recruits in, which is true."

Reamer, an oft-injured defensive back his first two seasons at Alabama, moved to linebacker upon Saban's arrival. He's started each of the last two seasons at Sam (strong side) linebacker and is also one of the team's top special-teams players. The Hoover, Alabama, native's shining moment came in a 22–3 win over Ole Miss on October 10. He blocked a punt and also forced and recovered a fumble on the same play, with both big plays setting up Alabama scores.

"It was something I took personally," Reamer said. "I have to get out there and go to work every day, and prove I can be a part of this team. It's been something I've heard since I came to Alabama, that I wouldn't play much."

Also key members of Alabama's dominating defense are Washington (defensive end), Anders (linebacker), and Johnson (nickel cornerback). Unlike many of the others, Washington was a big-time recruit but battled injuries and position changes to become one of the Crimson Tide's defensive stalwarts. He started most of the 2007 season as an undersized nose tackle, but moved to end the following season to make

Football is truly a team game; without all 11 players playing at their best, the team as a whole cannot have success. Eryk Anders typifies the unsung heroes of the 2009 Crimson Tide, recording 56 tackles from his Jack linebacker spot and tying for second on the team with five regular-season sacks.

Colin Peek was a reliable target at tight end for Alabama in 2009, finishing fourth on the team in receiving during the regular season with 24 catches and a pair of touchdowns. His only other full season of college football was in 2007, when he played in all 12 games for Georgia Tech.

way for eventual All-American Terrence Cody.

Anders was a late addition to the 2005 signing class, and through his first three seasons appeared as if he might not ever play a significant role for the Crimson Tide. But the 6-foot-2, 227-pound Texan finally found a role as a pass-rushing specialist in 2008, and has started every game this season at Jack linebacker. "Coach Saban says it's not the size of the dog, it's the fight in the dog," fellow linebacker McClain said. "Eryk is a fighter, no matter how big he is. He finds a way to get the job done."

And then there's Johnson, who was the whipping boy for fans and opposing offenses alike for much of the 2007, 2008, and 2009 seasons. His penchant for allowing big passing plays made him among the most unpopular Alabama players in recent memory. But Saban stuck with Johnson, and he has been rewarded. He leads the team in

pass break-ups, including a memorable sequence against South Carolina where he knocked down three consecutive passes in the end zone.

"I think back to when he was a sophomore and we were playing Florida State and (media) were saying, 'Don't you have anybody else you could put in there?'" Saban said. "We believed in the guy and worked with him. And he worked really hard himself and has become a really good player, who is very confident in what he is doing."

Davis is another interesting case, who was all but an afterthought in recruiting because he played at tiny Sparta Academy, a private school in south Alabama. But he was blessed with a 6-foot-7 frame, and eventually was able to build himself up in the weight room into a 300-pound specimen who has started two straight years at right tackle.

(opposite) Though it appeared he might never see meaningful game action at Alabama, Anders kept working and never gave up. His special teams experience in 2008 made him hungry enough to become a regular contributor in 2009. (above) The offensive line only returned two starters in 2009, leaving it as a major question mark heading into the season. With leadership from seniors like Drew Davis, however, the unit was one of the most consistent in the SEC, opening up holes for the ground-based offense and providing quality protection for Greg McElroy.

Peek almost signed with the Crimson Tide out of high school in 2005, but went to Georgia Tech instead. He transferred to Alabama prior to the 2008 season, and has made the tight end position a weapon again in the passing game in his first season after gaining eligibility.

Upchurch was perhaps the biggest-name recruit on this list, a Parade All-American in 2004. But a series of ankle and shoulder injuries robbed him of some of his speed and quickness, and he's settled into a key role as a third-down back, noted for his abilities as a receiver and pass-blocker.

Selman is paying his own way at Alabama as a walk-on, but that hasn't kept him from excelling on the field. In two years as the Crimson Tide's long-snapper, he has yet to commit a bad snap.

But perhaps no player on the Alabama roster ha undergone more of a transformation than Tiffin, whe endured one of the all-time nightmare games in Crimsor Tide history as a freshman in 2006. He missed three field goals and an extra point in a game Alabama lost by a single point in overtime at Arkansas.

Calls to replace Tiffin have been periodic over the years, but he's held onto the job. He's been dynamite as a senior, and is one of three finalists for the Lou Groza Award, given to the country's top kicker.

"I think you'd be hard-pressed to find a guy who's never had a bad game that's done this long enough," Tiffin said. "I just think it's a natural part of the process and I always felt like I had the talent to be a good kicker I overcame a lot of obstacles, and now I think I'm per forming close to what I'm capable of doing." •

(opposite) A big heart is certainly needed to succeed in football, and Roy Upchurch doubtlessly has one of the biggest. After neck surgery ended his year in 2008, the senior came back to provide some of the most memorable moments of 2009. (above) Long snapper Brian Selman has not had one bad snap in his two years manning the position.